U.S. Immigration:
A Policy Analysis

**U.S. Immigration:
A Policy Analysis**

a Public Issues paper of
The Population Council

Charles B. Keely

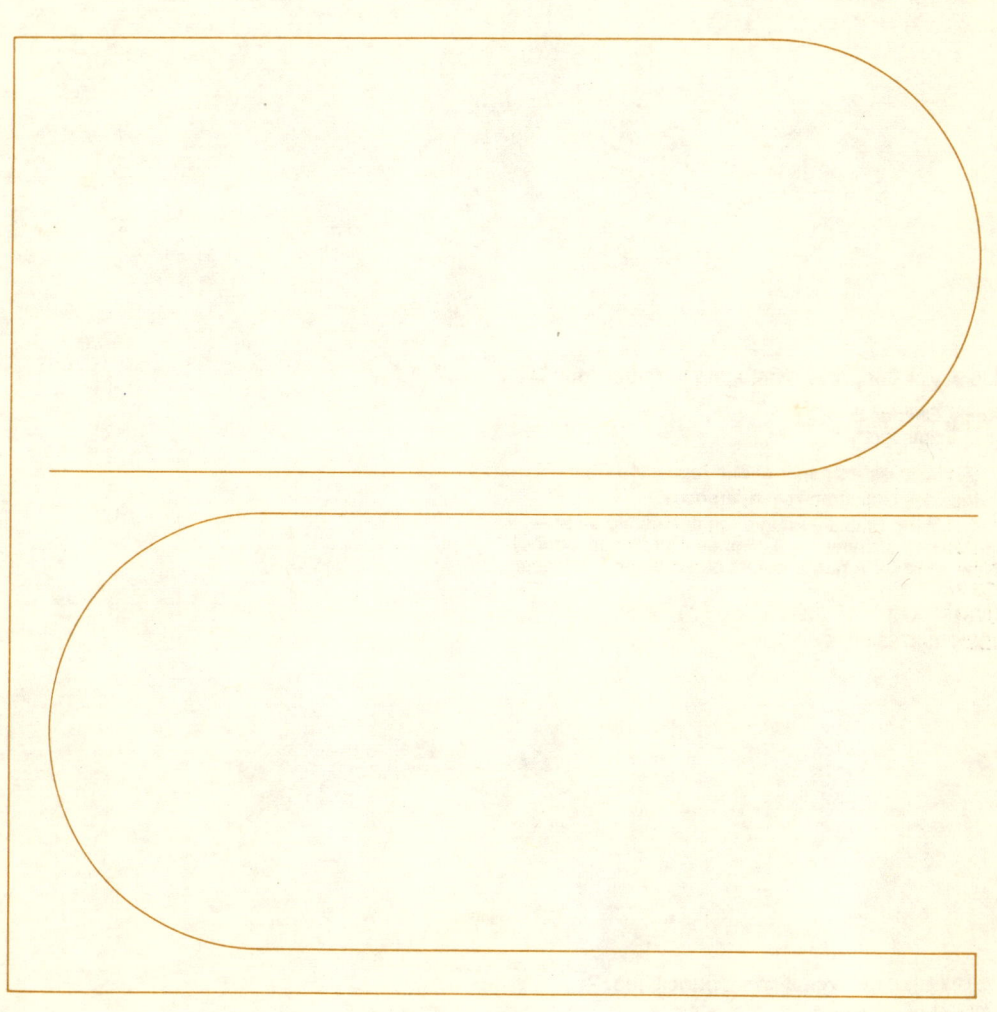

The Population Council
One Dag Hammarskjold Plaza
New York, N.Y. 10017   U.S.A.

Library of Congress Cataloging in Publication Data

Keely, Charles B
  U.S. immigration.

  (A public issues paper of the Population Council)
  Includes bibliographical references.
  1. United States—Emigration and immigration—History.   I. Title.   II. Series: Population Council, New York.   A public issues paper of the Population Council.
JV6450.K43   325.73   79-12261
ISBN 0-87834-039-4

©1979 by the Population Council, Inc.
All rights reserved
Printed in the United States of America

Acknowledgments

This presentation has benefited from the suggestions, criticisms, and help of many individuals. I owe a particular debt to Leonard Mayhew and Stephen Salyer. In addition, I thank Michael Todaro, Paul Demeny, Barnett Baron, James Bausch, Roger Hansen, Linda Ainsworth, Robert Heidel, and Carolina Pinto for their comments and contributions.

My hope is that this Public Issues paper stimulates discussion and provides useful options for US immigration policies. If it succeeds, my debt is that much greater to all who have contributed to my thinking on immigration questions and to those who devoted time and effort to this project.

CHARLES B. KEELY
New York City
March 1979

Contents

Foreword ix

Introduction 1

Part 1 A History of Ambivalence 8
Free Movement, 1790–1874 8
Individual Minimal Requirements, 1875–1920 11
National Origins Quotas, 1921–1964 15
Family Reunion and Labor Needs, 1965–Present 19
Current Contexts of Immigration Policy 24

Part 2 Policy Approaches and Supporters 30
Adjusting Immigration to Labor Force Requirements 31
Controlling Population Growth 36
Maintaining Family Reunion and Refugee Resettlement 39

Part 3 Policy Issues 44
International Migration and Population Growth 46
Illegal Migration 50
Legal Immigration and the Labor Force 62
Family Reunion 65
Nonimmigrants and Adjustment of Status 66
Refugee Admittance 68
Pluralism 71

Conclusion 77

Notes 79

Foreword

Many readers tend to associate population research and policy with high fertility and related program issues. As important as these are, the study of population change, including its effects and alternative policy responses, is much broader. Indeed, from the perspective of many governments, the population question is less a matter of high fertility than of uncontrolled and unpredictable migration of people within or across national borders. Policymakers, in both developed and developing nations, want to know more about the extent, causes, and consequences of such movement in order to respond in reasonable ways.

The Population Council is aware that reliable information upon which to base migration policymaking is scarce. In our Center for Policy Studies and through our International Programs activities, we are attempting to answer questions about the size and composition of migrant flows, their effects at family, community, and national levels, and the actions that governments might take to alter or ameliorate the negative impacts of such movements and effects.

As in other areas of public decision making, however, migration policies are often made without benefit of anything approaching accurate information. In this respect, the United States is not different from nations with less elaborate statistical apparatus. Under these circumstances, a disinterested presentation of historical trends and competing political considerations may provide the most feasible context within which to discuss policy adjustments. Such is the belief and approach underlying this Public Issues paper.

As a nation of immigrants, the United States is deeply affected by the topic of immigration. Yet, as the paper notes, the nation's policies in this area resist scientific formulation. The subject is equally sensitive in many other countries, affecting population growth, the supply of labor, family relationships, and aspects of personal liberty. For these reasons we hope that this presentation will be of interest to readers outside as well as within the United States, even though its specific focus is the American experience. As the paper makes clear, although migration policies may be decided by national governments, their impacts are increasingly international.

GEORGE ZEIDENSTEIN
New York City

**U.S. Immigration:
A Policy Analysis**

Introduction

Immigration strikes deep chords and cuts across many interests in the United States. It speaks directly to the core questions of what kind of society Americans have built and want in the future. It is a complex issue with ramifications for a broad range of domestic and foreign policies.

Immigration has emerged periodically in US history as a political issue, although the circumstances responsible for motivating our attention have changed through the years. In Part 1 of this paper we examine some of the crosscurrents and themes that underlie immigration policy and attempt to demonstrate how their influence remains potent in the way contempory policies are formulated and discussed.

Because we think of ourselves as a "nation of immigrants" and because the issues involved are so central to the nature of American society, effective analysis of immigration measures requires some understanding of organized political pressures affecting the consideration of options. For this reason, Part 2 considers the major positions and their supporters within the present debate. The purpose here is not to "take sides," but rather to provide the reader with a sufficient grasp of *Realpolitik* in this area to assess policy options realistically.

Finally, in Part 3 of the paper, we turn to the diverse range of policies and programs that together comprise "immigration policy." Although necessarily complex—some say incoherent—these overlapping measures determine the posture against which our objectives for immigration policy, both foreign and domestic, will be judged. The underlying assumption of this paper, illustrated by the options presented in Part 3, is that immigration measures can and should be made a more consistent and workable package. The concluding section is intended to enable the reader to understand and evaluate the range of proposals that has been presented to "reform" immigration policy.

The time is right for a presentation of this kind, as momentum for reconsideration of immigration measures has been building steadily in recent years.

In its 1971 Interim Report,[1] the Commission on Population Growth and the American Future noted that immigration accounts for between 20 and 25 percent of US population growth. As our rate of natural increase—the growth in population due to excess of births over deaths—declines, a steady number of immigrants will constitute a larger proportion of a declining overall growth. Even now immigration is a significant factor in population dynamics.

In its Final Report in 1972,[2] the Commission also took note of "illegal migration,"[3] a subject of increasing concern in the United States during the 1970s. It has been variously labeled a large and growing problem, a "vast and silent invasion,"[4] and the "hidden population bomb."[5] It has prompted calls from government, business groups, organized labor, and a variety of organizations for policies and programs to deal with undocumented migrants presently in the country and for more stringent measures to prevent the entry of others.

Broad awareness of the issues of illegal migration and population growth has run parallel to the continued concern of government officials and private sector groups over other immigration-related matters, including refugee policies, the relationship between immigration and manpower policy, the foreign policy implications of immigration policy, and foreign-student and exchange-visitor programs.

As a result, the Carter Administration has established an Interagency Task Force on Immigration, while Congress has created a 16-member Select Commission on Immigration and Refugee Policy. The administration did not originally support the idea of a Select Commission; in fact, the President had announced the Interagency Task Force in August 1977 as an alternative. The mandate of the Task Force was to review immigration legislation and to make legislative recommendations for Executive initiatives within 18 months. The Task Force director and staff, however, were not assembled until the summer of 1978. By that time, the administration had changed its position and supported the Select Commission, which had strong backing from the House and Senate Judiciary Committees, whose jurisdiction includes immigration legislation. Meanwhile, the Interagency Task Force became a lame duck with a small budget and a self-imposed deadline of January 1979 for submitting its report. It has concentrated on providing background papers that would be useful to the Select Commission's deliberations.

The Select Commission is composed of four members of the Judiciary Committee of each house of Congress, the Secretaries of State, Labor, and Health, Education, and Welfare, the Attorney General, and four public members appointed by the President, one of whom will chair the Commission. The Commission's mandate is broad: to review and recommend legislative changes in immigration and refugee policy and its administration.

(c) "It shall be the duty of the Commission to study and evaluate ... existing laws, policies, and procedures governing the admission of immigrants and refugees to the United States and to make such administrative and legislative recommendations to the President and to the Congress as are appropriate.

(d) In particular, the Commission shall—

(1) conduct a study and analysis of the effect of the provisions of the Immigration and Nationality Act (and administrative interpretations thereof) on (A) social, economic, and political conditions in the United States; (B) demographic trends; (C) present and projected unemployment in the United States; and (D) the conduct of foreign policy;

(2) conduct a study and analysis of whether and to what extent the Immigration and Nationality Act should apply to the Commonwealth of Puerto Rico, the Virgin Islands, Guam, American Samoa, the Northern Mariana Islands, and the other territories and possessions of the United States;

(3) review, and make recommendations with respect to, the numerical limitations (and exemptions therefrom) of the Immigration and Nationality Act on the admission of permanent resident aliens;

(4) assess the social, economic, political, and demographic impact of previous refugee programs and review the criteria for, and the numerical limitations on, the admission of refugees to the United States;

(5) conduct a comprehensive review of the provisions of the Immigration and Nationality Act and make legislative recommendations to simplify and clarify such provisions...."[6]

A two-to-three-year review process will likely precede enactment of measures constituting a comprehensive legislative package, although passage of some reforms may come sooner and debate across the wide range of issues should intensify in coming months.

No policy will be acceptable to all, nor can any single overview touch all issues or satisfy all readers. This presentation represents the views of one observer of immigration matters. It seeks to be fair and accurate in its presentation of history and of competing points of view. Its advantage, perhaps, derives from the author's liberty to proceed unencumbered by political exigencies that can force compromise of both analysis and recommendations. Because the views expressed here are not meant to represent those held by any interest group or organization, including the Population Council, and because as a nation we are still at an early stage of policy review and reformulation, this Public Issues paper should be read as presenting one among many possible responses to our immigration policy requirements, by no means the final word.

1 A History of Ambivalence

My opinion, with respect to immigration, is that except of useful mechanics and some particular descriptions of men or professions, there is no need of encouragement, while the policy or advantage of its taking place in a body (I mean the settling of them in a body) may be much questioned; for, by so doing, they retain their language, habits and principles (good and bad) which they bring with them.[7]

GEORGE WASHINGTON TO JOHN ADAMS

We are the Romans of the modern world, the great assimilating people.[8]

OLIVER WENDELL HOLMES

The United States has always been of two minds about new immigrants. On the one hand, the country has historically been a refuge, a place of new beginnings, accepting and even recruiting new settlers to build the nation and its economy. On the other hand, the theme of protectionism has found recurrent expression in apprehension over the capacity of the culture and economy to absorb newcomers, in the desire to limit labor market competition and assure minimal health standards, and even in nativism and racist theories. The history of immigration policy is a dialectic of these two themes of acceptance and protection.

Free Movement, 1790–1874

Before 1875, American policy is best characterized as neutral, neither encouraging nor discouraging immigration. Except for the Alien Act of 1798, which authorized the President for two years to deport any alien he considered dangerous to the United States, and which was not renewed, no federal legislation was enacted to restrict immigration or permit deportation of aliens.

The widespread use of the word "immigrant" appears to date from 1817.[9] During the colonial era and the early years of the Republic, settlers were referred to as "emigrants": they migrated *from* somewhere. After 1817 they were perceived as migrating *to* a new nation, as part of a great experiment. Freedom and seemingly boundless opportunity invited people through the Golden Door. In terms of national survival, growth, and development, the immigrant was a blessing and a confirmation of the nation. But behind the blessing some saw danger. Benjamin Franklin "had misgivings about Germans because of their clannishness, their little knowledge of English, the German press, and the increasing need of interpreters. Speaking of the latter he said, 'I suppose in a few years they will also be necessary in the Assembly, to tell one-half of our legislators what the other half say.'" The stereotype of the rowdy Irish in tumbledown shanties, a "low and squalid class of people, who ... keep ... the surroundings in a filthy and disgusting condition," was born during this period.[10]

Historically, the United States has both encouraged immigrants and expressed concern about the country's ability to absorb them culturally and economically.

This period brought the first flowering of nativism, an "intense opposition to an internal minority on the ground of its foreign (*i.e.*, 'un-American') connections."[11] Nativism's roots long antedate the new nation. Early America's strongest antiforeign tradition originated with the anti-Catholicism of the Protestant Reformation. Provocative rhetoric (e.g., Rome: the Whore of Babylon) and tales of lascivious priests and nuns were widespread. Deep-rooted anti-Catholicism took on nativist overtones as Catholics were perceived as threatening foreign agents. "The Roman pontiff loomed in English eyes as the great foreign tyrant, menacing the nation and its constitution; his followers had the aspect of a fifth column."[12]

A second nativist tradition was the fear of foreign radicals, expressed in the Alien Act of 1798. Although America was created by revolution, Americans have interpreted their revolution as perfecting an existing social order with little social transformation. Other revolutions toppled an old order and built on its ruins; but egalitarian America, with its traditions of social and economic mobility, spawned less desperate politics than class-ridden Europe.

In addition, the very poor were considered dangerous, a potential source of European-style radicalism. The typical economic condition of each new lot of immigrants, therefore, was seen as un-American. The question was raised with each new wave whether their poverty and lifestyle were signs of inherent inability to become American.

> American nativism has been anti-Catholic and antiradical while fostering a cult of Anglo-Saxonism.

The antiradical and anti-Catholic traditions defined what America was not and must not become. A third tradition defined what America was and should be: Anglo-Saxon. "Providence has been pleased to give this one connected country to one united people—a people descended from the same ancestors, speaking the same language, professing the same religion, attached to the same principles of government, very similar in their manners and customs."[13] Although not strictly accurate, *The Federalist* enunciated the Anglo-Saxon tradition.

The first period of US history, then, was marked by substantial immigration and legislative inaction on the federal level but, in addition, by the development of a nativism that would later play so large a part in immigration policy. In this period, manpower needs for America's economic development and expansion overshadowed the antiforeign animus. Figure 1 and the accompanying highlights (pp. 12–13) interpret changes in immigration levels from 1825 to 1975.[14]

The absence of federal legislation, however, does not mean there was no desire to restrict immigration. Opposition to immigrants was expressed during the 1850s in the Know-Nothing movement and in California's anti-Chinese legislation. The Know-Nothing movement was able to form a coalition based on ethnic and religious bias, worker resentment of competition, and Southern fears of Northern population growth and political power. Successful at the polls in the 1850s, the movement faded with the onset of the Civil War.

We must not forget that this era also included continuation of the slave trade. The regional differences on this issue were resolved in a constitutional compromise of 1787. Article I, Section 9 still reads: "The migration or importation of such persons as any of the states now existing shall think proper to admit, shall not be prohibited by the Congress prior to the year 1808 but a tax or duty may be imposed on such importation, not exceeding ten dollars for each person." Although Congress forbade the slave trade after 1808, it continued. Only with Lincoln's Emancipation Proclamation did the slave trade end in the United States.

Individual Minimal Requirements, 1875–1920

In 1876 the Supreme Court ruled that state laws regulating immigration were unconstitutional. The Court held that Congress alone has the power to regulate immigration under Article I, Section 8 of the Constitution, which empowers Congress "to regulate commerce with foreign nations, and among the several states, and with Indian tribes."

Following the Court ruling, Congress exercised its constitutional prerogatives by enacting protectionist legislation aimed primarily at individual characteristics of immigrants, but not at restricting total volume. Of the dozen or so major immigration laws passed between 1875 and 1920, about three-quarters were primarily aimed at excluding persons with diseases, criminal records, and unacceptable moral standards or political beliefs.[15] Chronic

Most major immigration acts passed during 1875–1920 sought to exclude the sick, the criminal, and those with unacceptable morals or politics.

Highlights of Events to Interpret Changes in Immigration Levels, 1825–1975

1825–1874

1830s Sharp increase in volume of immigration; beginning of Irish domination of immigrant stream

Late 1840s–early 1850s: Heavy Irish and German immigration

1861–65 Civil War. Lull in nativist movements.

1872 Major decline in foreign (esp. British) capital investment in US

1875–1920

1875 First federal law excluding criminals and prostitutes from admission

1876 Supreme Court ruling that power to legislate on immigration rests exclusively with Congress

1880s Beginning of "new immigration" (from southern and eastern Europe)

1882 First Chinese exclusion act

1885 First contract labor law

1893–97 Recession

1896 New immigration constituted majority of total immigrants

1900–1914 Peak levels of immigration

1907 Largest single year of immigration: 1,285,349 persons admitted

1914–17 World War I

1917 Literacy test requirement

1921–1964

1921 First quota act (3 percent of foreign born of each nationality as enumerated in 1910 Census)

1924 Second quota act (2 percent of foreign born of each nationality as enumerated in 1890 Census until 1929. After 1929, quota of a country stood in the same relation to 150,000 as inhabitants of US of that ethnic origin to total US inhabitants in 1920 Census, with minimum quota of 100).

1930s Depression

1941–45 World War II

1945–53 Special legislation for postwar admissions of displaced persons and war brides

1952 McCarran-Walter Act

1953 Refugee Relief Act

1958 Hungarian refugees permitted to adjust to immigrant status

1965–Present

1965–68 Transitional phasing out of quota system

1968 About 100,000 adjustments of status of Cuban refugees before imposition of 120,000 ceiling on Western Hemisphere visa issuance

1969–75 Full provisions of 1965 Immigration Act in force

1978 Worldwide ceiling of 290,000 becomes law

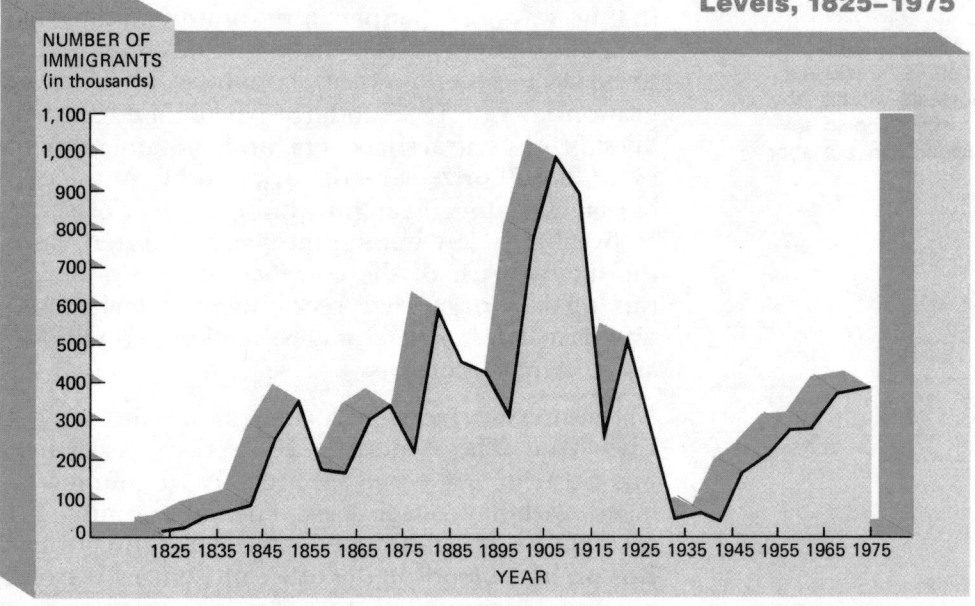

Figure 1
US Immigration Levels, 1825–1975

alcoholics, felons, anarchists, professional beggars, polygamists, prostitutes, and persons with tuberculosis, epilepsy, and mental illnesses or retardation were excluded by law.

The legislation of this period also sought to protect American labor. Organized labor pressed for prohibition of contract laborers, "servile classes" used for strike breaking. At first, labor did not advocate a broad restrictionist policy. "We are not objecting to immigration that is voluntary," declared the president of the Amalgamated Association of Iron and Steel Workers as late as 1892.[16] But, particularly under American Federation of Labor president Samuel Gompers, labor became increasingly restrictionist with the depression of 1893–97.

The resulting US policy was somewhat contradictory. The would-be immigrant had to demonstrate that he was not a pauper or destitute, but also that he had no job prospects that could be construed as prearranged (i.e., no contract in hand). The immigration laws of 1885 and 1887 prohibited the admission of contract laborers, and the amendment of 1888 authorized the deportation of contract labor law violators if caught within one year of entry. In practice, many immigrants were admitted, since the main thrust of the contract labor prohibition was against organized recruitment, which could undercut US laborers' wages, working conditions, and organizing efforts.

> A would-be immigrant had to prove he was not destitute, yet his job prospects could not include contract labor.

Nativism resurfaced following a lull during the Civil War. The American Protective Association was born in Iowa in 1887, mainly to counter alleged Catholic conspiracies. The Immigration Restriction League developed out of a meeting of five Boston blue bloods in the office of Charles Warren, a noted constitutional historian. The league advocated adoption of a literacy test that would reduce the number and limit the national origins of the "new immigration" from southern and eastern Europe. The literacy test requirement was vetoed by Presidents Cleveland and Taft, but was finally passed over President Wilson's second veto in 1917.

> The panoply of scientific racism would be laughable were it not for the immense harm caused in its name.

The restrictionist movement increasingly appealed to "scientific racism"—a series of highly questionable assumptions, twistings of Darwin's theory of evolution and its counterpart, the Social Darwinism of Herbert Spencer, and an alchemist's smorgasbord of "measurement" techniques from cephalic indexes to somatic types. The panoply of scientific racism would be laughable today were it not for the immense harm caused in its name in the twentieth century, particularly in Nazi Germany. This framework took hold and served as the conventional wisdom of the day. It provided the foundation for the 42-volume report issued in 1911 by the Joint Commission on Immigration, named after its chairman, Senator William P. Dillingham of Vermont, which purported to demonstrate the inferiority of the immigrant "races" and blamed them for a host of ills. The full impact of the Dillingham Commission was to be felt in the national origins quota system of the 1920s.

The excludable classes prohibited by the legislation of 1882 included a whole nation, the Chinese. Chinese exclusion, extended by the "Gentlemen's Agreement" of 1907 to Japanese and ultimately in 1917 to all Asians, was clearly not aimed at an individual's qualities, but referred to a whole group. Chinese exclusion seems to have been a labor protection measure, with a heavy dose of racism so intertwined that it is hard to separate the two. Chinese exclusion foreshadowed in both substance and rhetoric the national origins quota policy.

Nevertheless, while the restrictionists were trying to develop a consensus to limit immigration numerically and the mechanisms to reduce or exclude whole groups on "racial" grounds, immigration continued to grow. The volume of immigration (see Figure 1), its changing composition, and the xenophobia accompanying World War I led to the success of the nativist viewpoint.

Chinese exclusion was extended to Japanese in 1907 by the Gentlemen's Agreement, and to all Asians in 1917.

The literacy tests instituted in 1917 set the stage for the national origins quota acts of the 1920s. These acts, passed in 1921 and 1924, put a ceiling on total immigration and reserved fixed proportions of visas based on the national origins of the US population, thus favoring northern and western European nations in the visa distribution.

The national origins quota system remained the foundation of US immigration policy until 1965, although there were periodic challenges to the concept. The granting of a small quota to China, a

National Origins Quotas, 1921–1964

15

The national origins quota system developed in the 1920s favored immigrants from northern and western Europe.

wartime ally, in 1943 was an acknowledgment of the diplomatic embarrassment of Asian exclusion. The various special programs and legislation after World War II to accommodate refugees and displaced persons for humanitarian and political stabilization reasons, along with war brides and grooms, made it clear that the quota system was not in fact completely determining the ethnic mix of immigrants.

A congressional review of immigration law begun in 1948 resulted in the McCarran-Walter Act of 1952, the first codification of immigration and nationality law. Passed over President Truman's veto, the Act reaffirmed the quota concept. Although the recently ended war reduced the acceptability of racial inferiority arguments, the concept of assimilability was used to justify favoring natives of countries with cultural and historical ties to the United States. Asian exclusion was dropped, but persons of Asian ancestry were treated differently from others for immigration purposes. For example, a second-generation Brazilian of Japanese ancestry was to be counted against Japan's small quota, whereas a second-generation Brazilian of Italian ancestry was treated as a Brazilian, not an Italian.

The McCarran-Walter Act also included a preference system for distributing visas within each country's quota allotment. Although seldom used by immigrants from large-quota countries, the preference system reserved half the visas for use by workers and their dependents, while other preferences were assigned to family members of citizens and of permanent resident aliens. Table 1 illustrates the preference system of the McCarran-Walter Act.

Passage of a new quota system, however, did not mark the end of the tradition of accepting immigrants. President Truman proclaimed that aspect of American tradition in his veto message:

**Table 1
Preference System of the Immigration and Nationality Act of 1952**

1. First preference: Highly skilled immigrants whose services are urgently needed in the United States, and the spouse and children of such immigrants.
    60 percent plus any not required for second and third preferences.

2. Second preference: Parents of citizens over the age of 21, and unmarried sons and daughters of US citizens.
    30 percent plus any not required for first and third preferences.

3. Third preference: Spouse and unmarried sons and daughters of an alien lawfully admitted for permanent residence.
    20 percent plus any not required for first or second preference.

4. Fourth preference: Brothers, sisters, and married sons and daughters of US citizens, and any accompanying spouse and children.
    50 percent of numbers not required for first three preferences.

5. Nonpreference: Applicants not entitled to one of the above preferences.
    50 percent of numbers not required for first three preferences, plus any not required for fourth.

Source: Department of State, Bureau of Security and Consular Affairs, *Report of the Visa Office* (Washington, D.C.: US Government Printing Office, 1968), p. 68.

"[The] quota system—always based upon assumptions at variance with our American ideals—is long since out of date. . . . The greatest vice of the present system, however, is that it discriminates, deliberately and intentionally, against many of the peoples of the world. . . .

The idea behind this policy was, to put it boldly, that Americans with English or Irish names were better people and better citizens than Americans with Italian or Greek or Polish names. . . . Such a concept is utterly unworthy of our traditions and our ideals. It violates the great political doctrine of the Declaration of Independence that 'all men are created equal.' . . .

It repudiates our basic religious concepts, our belief in the brotherhood of man. . . .

It is incredible to me that, in this year of 1952, we should again be enacting into law such a slur on the patriotism, the capacity, and the decency of a large part of our citizenry."[17]

Although the McCarran-Walter Act reaffirmed the quota system, exceptions to the racial and nationality criteria were often made to admit refugees and displaced persons.

The aims of the nativists were partially achieved during this period. Figure 1 clearly indicates the overall decline in immigration. To be sure, the Depression and World War II were at least as responsible as the ceiling placed on immigrant visas; however, limitations on immigration became almost universally accepted. There has been no serious proposal to return to a policy of unlimited entry controlled only by requiring minimal health and moral standards that characterized the period of 1875–1920. In that sense, US policy could be labeled "restrictionist"; yet in terms of overall admissions and subsequent opportunity for citizenship, American policy continues to be very generous in comparison with other countries.

The nativists' aim to reduce the number of undesirable aliens on racial or nationality criteria was less successful. Because of the admission of refugees and displaced persons, the national origins composition of post–World War II immigrants did not conform to the national origins quotas. Although the quota policy was reaffirmed by the McCarran-Walter Act, refugee resettlement—and therefore deviations from the policy—persisted as World War II refugee resettlement continued during the 1950s, augmented by the Hungarian refugee movement later in the decade.

Family Reunion and Labor Needs, 1965–Present

After 1952 presidential platforms of both parties called for immigration reform. President Eisenhower echoed Truman's call for a revision of immigration law, especially the quota system, in his 1953 State of the Union Message. Indeed, he sent a special message on immigration reform or mentioned it in his State of the Union Message to every Congress (83rd to 86th) that sat during his two terms as President. President Kennedy also made a major effort to reform immigration. The result of hearings on the bill prepared by the Kennedy Administration was a much-altered set of immigration amendments signed into law by President Johnson in 1965. These amendments to the McCarran-Walter Act immediately ended the Asian discrimination provisions and mandated a phasing out of the national origins quota system by 1968. The bill also contained a new preference system for the distribution of visas.

The Immigration Act of 1965 also introduced two innovations: (1) a ceiling was put on visas for immigration from the Western Hemisphere, and (2) all nonrelative and nonrefugee immigrants were required to obtain a labor clearance certifying that American workers were not available for their jobs and that the immigrants would not lower prevailing wages and working conditions.

The basic policy as of 1 July 1968 specified that 120,000 visas could be granted to persons born in the Western Hemisphere and 170,000 to persons born in all other countries. The 170,000 visas for the Eastern Hemisphere were to be distributed according to seven preferences, as illustrated in Table 2, but natives of no single country were to receive more than 20,000 visas annually. Those who received a worker preference (third or sixth preference) and nonpreference immigrants needed a labor certification before receiving a visa. For Western Hemisphere immigrants, on the other hand, there was no preference system and no country limit of 20,000 visas; however, a labor certification was required for all visa applicants except immediate family members of US citizens and permanent resident aliens. In 1976, the law was changed so that the Western Hemisphere provisions conformed to the Eastern Hemisphere selection system. The only difference in the parallel but separate systems was that the overall ceiling on annual visa allotments was kept at 120,000 for the Western Hemisphere and 170,000 for the rest of the world.

In October 1978, President Carter signed into law a worldwide ceiling bill. This bill combined the two ceilings into a single, worldwide ceiling of 290,000 visas to be distributed annually, with no change in the preference system and other procedures. Table 3 presents a synopsis of the 1952 McCarran-Walter Act—the basic immigration code—(pp. 22–23) and additional amendments contained in the Acts of 1965, 1976, and 1978. The effect of each of these steps in the development of a worldwide policy has been a trend toward a larger proportion of immigrants from southern Europe, Asia, and Latin America. These changes in law, and the even greater changes in regulations for implementing the law, have resulted in an extremely complicated application process. One result is growing dissatisfaction with a system that, in substance and especially in operation, favors the educated and wealthy, who can maneuver themselves or hire guides to take them through the bureaucratic jungle and into the United States.

As of 1978, a worldwide ceiling permits 290,000 visas to be distributed annually, and those seeking a work preference also require labor certification.

**Table 2
Preference System of the Immigration Act of 1965**

1. First preference: Unmarried sons and daughters of US citizens.
    Not more than 20 percent.

2. Second preference: Spouse and unmarried sons and daughters of an alien lawfully admitted for permanent residence.
    20 percent plus any not required for first preference.

3. Third preference: Members of the professions and scientists and artists of exceptional ability.
    Not more than 10 percent.

4. Fourth preference: Married sons and daughters of US citizens.
    10 percent plus any not required for first three preferences.

5. Fifth preference: Brothers and sisters of US citizens.[a]
    24 percent plus any not required for first four preferences.

6. Sixth preference: Skilled and unskilled workers in occupations for which labor is in short supply in the United States.
    Not more than 10 percent.

7. Seventh preference: Refugees to whom conditional entry or adjustment of status may be granted.
    Not more than 6 percent.

8. Nonpreference: Any applicant not entitled to one of the above preferences.
    Any numbers not required for preference applicants.

[a]Amended in 1976 to require US citizens conferring benefit to be over 21 years of age.
Source: See Table 1.

Table 3
Major Provisions of Recent US Immigration Acts

Provisions	1952	1965[c]	1976	1978
Ceilings				
EH	158,561	170,000	170,000	None
WH	None	120,000	120,000	None
Total	158,561 plus	290,000	290,000	290,000
Exempt from Ceilings				
EH	Spouse and children of adult US citizens	Parents, spouse, and children of adult US citizens	Parents, spouse, and children of adult US citizens	Parents, spouse, and children of adult US citizens
WH	No ceiling	Parents, spouse, and children of adult US citizens	Parents, spouse, and children of adult US citizens	Parents, spouse, and children of adult US citizens
Country Quotas or Ceilings				
EH	Proportionate to 1920 US ethnic composition	20,000	20,000	20,000
WH	None	None	20,000	20,000
Preference System[a]				
EH	4 preferences	7 preferences	7 preferences[d]	7 preferences[d]
WH	None	None	7 preferences[d]	7 preferences[d]

Provisions	1952	1965[c]	1976	1978
Labor Certification				
EH	By complaint[b]	3rd, 6th, non-preference	3rd, 6th, non-preference	3rd, 6th, non-preference
WH	By complaint[b]	All except immediate family of citizens and of permanent resident aliens	3rd, 6th, non-preference	3rd, 6th, non-preference

EH = Eastern Hemisphere   WH = Western Hemisphere

[a]See Tables 1 and 2. The percentages apply to the country ceilings in the 1952 Act, to hemisphere ceiling in 1965 and 1976, and the worldwide ceiling of 1978.

[b]No prior certification prescribed in 1952 Act. A complaint had to be lodged or an employer had to petition for 25 or more applicants before a Department of Labor review was initiated.

[c]Provisions listed refer to system as of 1968, after elimination of quota system of 1952 Act and imposition of Western Hemisphere ceiling.

[d]The 1976 Act provided that if a country met the 20,000 ceiling in any year, for the next year the preference proportions would apply to the 20,000 ceiling rather than the hemispheric or worldwide ceilings. This is to ensure that lower-preference and nonpreference applicants do not get squeezed out because of demands in the higher preferences. This provision is invoked in only a few countries where third preference demand is especially high.

Nevertheless, the 1965 Act and its successors have swung the pendulum away from nativism. The quota concept and its pseudo-intellectual baggage, scientific racism, were repudiated. Current law focuses on family reunion, acceptance of a fair share of refugees, and labor protection balanced against admitting persons with needed skills. Whether the law actually achieves these goals and whether, indeed, these goals are outdated are subjects of contention. But the 1965 Act continued the protectionist theme by initiating numerical ceilings on visa issuance to the Western Hemisphere.

Current Contexts of Immigration Policy

The historical tension between protection and acceptance is still evident.

The major topic of policy discussion is the demographic, socioeconomic, and foreign policy impacts of illegal migration.

The historical tension between the two immigration themes—protection and acceptance—is still evident. Those who wish to move to a more restrictive policy point to changes in the economy, resource base, and population—both in the United States and worldwide—that require changed goals for immigration, although there is no general agreement on what should be the paramount consideration in immigration policy. Some see the size and composition of the population as the major consideration. Others see employment requirements as the top priority in developing any new policy.

On the other hand, there are those who do not want more restrictive policies but at the same time believe that current policy, and particularly its administration, need revision. They also accept the fact that current national and international conditions call for a reexamination of immigration. They perceive the need to evaluate the population and labor force effects of immigration. They accept the general goals and policy framework of current immigration law but emphasize the need to perfect the mechanisms of distributing visas equitably, though in the national interest and without contributing to unsanctioned immigration.

Both sides call for review of immigration policy and law in light of new conditions and new interpretations of the role of immigration in population growth, the employment needs of a postindustrial economy, world refugee movements, brain drain, illegal migration, and so on. Despite the persistence of the two themes regarding immigration, there is no neat lineup of camps on specific issues. A position on one current immigration issue does not necessarily predict policy preference on others.

What, then, are the major issues under discussion? The main topic is undoubtedly illegal migration. Illegal migration has existed as long as there has been legislation regulating immigrant flows, but the current issue is the size of recent flows, the potential for greater flows, and the demographic, socioeconomic, and foreign policy impact of illegal migrants.

Strong "limits-to-growth" advocates pose questions about the effects of illegal and legal migration on current and future population growth. The time has come, according to these advocates, when immigration should make no net addition to the US population, since the world is running out of land and natural resources.

Others see legal and illegal migration as an economic problem for the United States. They desire a closer interaction between immigration and employment policies. Questions about the possibility and desirability of continued economic expansion lead to concerns about competition and the impact of international migration on the conditions of US workers and the civil rights of minorities. If the United States moves to a slow-growth or no-growth economy, to what degree can the country absorb additions to the current and future labor force?

This concern with labor force impact is reinforced by a change in the geographic origin of immigrants. For most of US history, the main source of immigrants and the focus of policy has been Europe. But some restrictionists did note the threat of the "back door," Latin America, and opposed exclusion of the Western Hemisphere countries from the quota system.[18] Indeed, the concern of some senators, notably Sam J. Ervin, Jr., James O. Eastland, Everett M. Dirksen, and Roman L. Hruska,[19] led to the first numerical ceiling on Western Hemisphere visas in 1965. Despite the ceiling, Latin American and Caribbean immigration, which was about 15 percent of total immigration between 1930 and 1960, constituted 41 percent between 1971 and 1974. The focus is now on the back door.

The populations of many Latin American countries have large proportions of young people. Even if high fertility and growth rates decline, substantial numbers of people already born will have little prospect for integration into their own labor force, even with the most optimistic of development forecasts. From a purely demographic viewpoint, the potential for immigration, legal and illegal, is great.

There is, in addition, concern over bilingual militancy among growing Spanish-origin groups. Parallels are drawn with French Canadian militancy, although Spanish-origin groups represent a variety of cultures and are widely dispersed in the United States. Language maintenance and use will continue to sharply focus the issue of pluralism.

The case of Mexico points up an additional context of current policy discussion: the foreign policy dimensions of immigration policy. The actual and potential links among migration, development, job creation, trade access, and Mexican oil and gas are clear. The issues of temporary labor transfers and economic development in many regions of the world dictate greater attention to the international effects of immigration policy.

Finally, there is the problem of developing coordinated international policy and action in regard to refugees. From the US viewpoint, this requires a mechanism for accepting refugees that is flexible and permits congressional monitoring of refugee movements within an overall immigration policy. At the same time, the US government has expressed the hope that other countries will show greater willingness to resettle refugees.

In sum, seven issues define the major areas for current immigration policy debate: illegal migration; population growth; the needs and absorptive capacity of the US labor force; the new geographic focus on immigration from Latin America and the Caribbean; the development of pluralism in the United States, especially in regard to the size and spreading influence of Spanish-origin groups and the substantive and symbolic importance of language maintenance; foreign relations on a bilateral and a multilateral level; and negotiating an international refugee resettlement policy and US administrative mechanisms for admitting refugees. A number of technical questions, including legislative language and administrative organization, are not discussed in this paper, not because they are unimportant—that is hardly the case—but because our focus is the broader policy choices involved in immigration and naturalization law.

The aforementioned immigration issues will probably be the main policy topics under discussion in the near future, particularly in the forum of the Select Commission on Immigration and Refugee Policy. Numerous interested parties will have access to the Commission as it reviews and develops recommendations for immigration legislation. Organized labor, voluntary refugee and immigrant aid agencies, ethnic organizations, population and environmental groups, and other private sector organizations will doubtless express their views on immigration issues. In addition, the Departments of State, Justice, and Labor have legislatively mandated roles in administering US immigration law. Each of these departments has its own views and interests concerning the shape of immigration policy and the regulations used to administer the laws. Ultimately, legislative recommendations must be reviewed by the appropriate committees of Congress, and legislation must be approved by Congress and the President. In short, there will be many actors with divergent interests and many forums for activity before major changes in immigration legislation become a reality.

Limits-to-growth concerns, ethnic-group relations, and US foreign policy in the hemisphere are major policy issues.

2 Policy Approaches and Supporters

This policy of supplying, by opposite and rival interests, the defects of better motives might be traced through the whole system of human affairs, private as well as public.[20]

JAMES MADISON,
Federalist Paper, Number 51

The interplay of individual and group interests benefits the republican form of government by keeping the majority from violating minority rights and a minority from usurping power. It is not surprising, therefore, that an issue of great substantive and symbolic importance to the nation stirs up "opposite and rival interests."

The three most salient policy perspectives vying for the attention of legislative reformers—adjusting immigration flows to labor force requirements, controlling population growth by limiting entry, and maintaining liberal family reunion and refugee admittance goals—provide useful categories within which to analyze immigration issues. These perspectives, even though not mutually exclusive, can justify very different policy outcomes depending on the priority they are assigned.

A wide range of individuals and groups line up in support of each of these perspectives. It is not uncommon, however, to find disagreement on particular issues among those emphasizing the same perspective, or to find advocates for a measure seeking to invoke more than one justification for their position. Still, certain interests do gravitate toward one or another of these perspectives.

These perspectives, and those who advocate them with greatest force, are described to clarify the connections between justifications, goals, and specific policy measures. The necessarily sketchy presentation of any particular group's interest or position is not intended to dismiss or discredit its broader purposes or specific stands. Rather, the intent is to provide a realistic backdrop against which to consider what, at the level of policy analysis, may appear to be equally plausible options.

Adjusting Immigration to Labor Force Requirements

The first policy perspective holds that, since most immigrants to the United States join the labor force, there should be greater consideration of the manpower impact of immigration. In fact, the Secretary of Labor, Ray Marshall, has proposed integrating employment and immigration policy. "I am particularly concerned that immigration and employment policies be closely coordinated. Obstacles to legal immigration encourage people to enter the country illegally. Since most of the people who come to the United States work, we should relate the number of legal immigrants to realistic labor market needs."[21]

The most developed approach to subordinating immigration policy to manpower needs is the report on immigration prepared by David S. North and Allen LeBel for the National Commission for Manpower Policy.[22] The Commission is composed of five Cabinet Secretaries (Defense, Agriculture, Commerce, Labor, and HEW), the administrator of the Veterans Administration, and seven other members from business, labor, state government, academia, and church groups. The authors describe their position on illegal migration as "restrictionist."[23] They not only support measures to end illegal migration, an almost universal goal in this country, but also reject expansion of temporary labor programs because of their labor market impact. On legal immigration, North and LeBel suggest a specific mechanism for coordination of immigration and manpower policy:

"Since most of the people who come to the United States work, we should relate the number of legal immigrants to realistic labor market needs."

"We recommend that the Congress give the Executive the discretion, each year, to set the immigration totals for the coming year within an arbitrary range of 300,000 to 500,000. . . . Although the Executive would announce the target early in the year, it would be free to increase it . . . but not to decrease it, as this would adversely affect persons who had made plans on the basis of the earlier announcement.

The annual total would be based on two, totally separate, calculations. The first would be the absorptive capacity of the nation, based primarily on the unemployment rate; the other consideration would be the nation's sense of responsibility for refugees and perhaps for other overseas political considerations."[24]

The Labor Department's insufficient data and resources make it nearly impossible to adjust immigration levels to regional and occupational needs.

North and LeBel thus translate the coordination concept into a specific program mechanism to gear immigration levels annually to unemployment rates. As the authors point out, however, one lesson of the labor certification program introduced in the 1965 Immigration Act is that a system to adjust immigration to the employment needs of regional labor markets and different occupations is difficult, if not impossible, given the current data bases and organizational resources of the Department of Labor and of state employment services. Further, even if employment requirements are the primary guide to immigrant selection, the presence of other accepted goals (as illustrated by North and LeBel's reference to refugee resettlement and foreign relations) can result in decisions that contradict employment goals. The recent experience of Canada is highly instructive. Canada uses a system that awards points to an applicant on the basis of family sponsorship, region of intended settlement, language abilities, and occupational needs. The goal of the system is to meet labor force needs, but the fact that an applicant can achieve the required number of points for admission, regardless of occupation, means that the desired results are not always achieved.

Toward a policy goal of family reunion the report is not as favorable. A basic premise of North and LeBel's recommendations is clearly stated: "There must be considerably more emphasis placed on the allocation of a publicly generated good, the immigrant visa, to meet the needs of society as a whole rather than those of individual members of society." Earlier they refer to "persons admitted for societal (as opposed to familial) reasons," and characterize the family reunion policies as having "an aura of nepotism." A particular target is the fifth preference of the 1965 Act: brothers and sisters of US citizens[25] (see Table 2).

As is to be expected, organized labor supports much of the stance that emphasizes employment policy. On illegal immigration, the AFL-CIO has consistently supported criminal sanctions for employers of undocumented aliens, an employment document based on the worker's Social Security number, increased border and labor law enforcement, US foreign aid geared to promoting employment in sending countries, and repeal of Tariff Code provisions that extend special customs treatment for goods produced in plants near the border and permit US companies to take advantage of low-wage workers in such operations as electronics assembly and garment work. The AFL-CIO favors amnesty for illegal migrants who entered the United States before 1970, but is ambiguous about how to treat those who entered after that date.[26]

On legal migration policy, organized labor continues its strong support of the goals in the 1965 Act. The change from organized labor's earlier restrictionist stand has not diluted its strong and persistent concern for protecting the American

To discourage illegal migration, organized labor consistently supports criminal sanctions for employers and increased border and labor law enforcement.

worker. Thus, it is unwilling to give up the labor certification procedure introduced in 1965, more because of its symbolic importance in reaffirming that immigration should not harm American labor than because organized labor views it as the best mechanism to achieve that goal.

Nevertheless, there is no unanimity in organized labor. The United Farm Workers, the International Ladies Garment Workers, and other union groups have supported full amnesty for illegal migrants, made efforts to organize undocumented workers, and generally opposed what they see as using illegal migrants and immigrants as scapegoats deflecting attention from labor law enforcement to improve working conditions. They also do not want illegal migration to be used as an excuse to pass laws restricting fundamental rights of workers, especially minority-group members who look or sound "foreign."

There are other supporters of coordinating immigration and manpower policy. Most notably, those who adopt the goal of population limitation ally themselves with the labor stance on the questions of illegal migration policy and on the selection procedures of a reduced legal immigrant flow. The major support is on the illegal migration question, where the goals of reduced population growth and the assumed negative labor force impacts of illegal migrants coincide. A recent pamphlet from Zero Population Growth, Inc., a citizens' organization that advocates a planned, voluntary stabilization of US and world population, presents a summary of the labor arguments:

"Illegal immigration is creating and perpetuating a subclass of workers deprived of civil and labor rights. . . . [U]ndocumented workers depress wages and working conditions in certain regions and fields of work. . . . In the Southwest, where

> Some labor groups fear that reactions against illegal migrants will lead to laws restricting the rights of US workers, especially ethnic minorities.

employers openly rely upon an endless supply of low-wage workers, illegal Mexican workers compete for jobs with legally resident Mexican-Americans.... In other labor markets, undocumented workers compete against native ethnic minorities including U.S. Blacks.... Usually pay and working conditions are too poor to attract legal U.S. residents. Legal residents often can turn to welfare payments when employers offer no better option, but undocumented workers are neither permitted nor inclined to seek welfare. If these lower-level jobs were upgraded in pay, working conditions and status, many could be filled by legal workers.... [I]t's still highly advantageous to hire [undocumented workers]. They are valued as hard workers, and some employers can get away without paying medical insurance, sick leave, overtime wages, unemployment compensation and Social Security payments. It's difficult for a native worker to compete with a deal like that. The availability of the large pool of illegal labor undermines labor union organizing among low-skilled workers."[27]

On legal immigration, ZPG calls for "tightening criteria for the Labor Department's imported labor certification program."[28]

Many Mexican-American groups join in opposition to expanding temporary worker programs, contending that temporary workers would only compete with Mexican-Americans, especially in the Southwest. This support, however, does not generally extend to the law enforcement proposals (e.g., sanctions against employers, broader police powers for border enforcement) that are usually included in programs aimed at reducing illegal migration, mainly because of the civil liberties concern that Mexicans and other ethnic groups will feel the brunt of uneven enforcement or outright discrimination.

Controlling Population Growth

A major and continuing result of changes in social consciousness has been concern about population growth and its environmental consequences. Currently, this concern is triggering a new look at the demographic consequences of immigration.

In 1971 the Commission on Population Growth and the American Future noted with surprise that immigration accounts for about 20 percent of overall annual growth. The Commission itself was divided on the topic of immigration: some members wished to reduce immigration by 10 percent annually over five years, to half its current level; others, bolstered by a paper prepared by Ansley J. Coale of Princeton University on the impact of current immigration on achievement of a no-growth or stationary population, held that immigration at present levels could be accommodated.[29] The Commission's final report made two proposals:

"The Commission recommends that Congress immediately consider the serious situation of illegal immigration and pass legislation which will impose civil and criminal sanctions on employers of illegal bordercrossers or aliens in an immigration status in which employment is not authorized.

The Commission recommends that immigration levels not be increased and that immigration policy be reviewed periodically to reflect demographic conditions and considerations."[30]

The Commission's recommendations reflected the division on the issue. The proposals not to raise current legal levels and to impose sanctions on employers of illegal migrants spoke to the concerns of those who wanted to reduce immigration. However, the phrasing on immigration was weak. There was not majority support to decrease the authorized level, so the compromise recommendation was not to increase it. In addition, the Commission report did not go into any detail on how to implement employer sanctions or on what constituted the criteria to be used "to reflect demographic conditions and considerations."

Nevertheless, immigration had been placed on the national population agenda. Since that time, it has received increasing attention. Zero Population Growth, currently the leading population-oriented advocacy group, provides a case study of the development of immigration as a population issue.

At its Boston convention in 1973, ZPG was faced with the good news that estimates of current fertility had dipped below replacement level; a major milestone of the organization had been achieved. But below-replacement fertility rates were only a first step. Because a large portion of the population was still young, below-replacement rates would have to be maintained for some time before a no-growth population could be achieved. Thus, ZPG had an interest in the continuation of low fertility to achieve its ultimate goal.

By 1973, then, it was evident that what ZPG had thought of as its pioneering fight to reduce fertility had become conventional wisdom and practice. The organization still had important program issues, but it raised the question of adding new ones. Immigration and the environment were two of the choices presented.

The major force on immigration in ZPG was John H. Tanton, a vice president of the organization in 1973 and its president in 1975–76. Under his leadership ZPG developed an effective immigration program focusing on the demographic impact of current immigration levels. Following the Population Commission's suggestion of a phased decrease in immigration, ZPG proposed in 1976 cutting immigration by more than half to an annual average of 150,000 (calculated on a five-year total of 750,000

ZPG proposes cutting immigration levels by more than half, hoping to achieve its goal of a zero-growth population by the year 2008.

to allow for annual fluctuations). (Although not specifically mentioned by ZPG, the 150,000 annual average would be approximately offset by current estimates of emigration, so that legal international migration would make no net addition to US population growth.) Its projections calculated 150,000 net additions from immigration as an acceptable level consonant with zero growth by the year 2008, with a population totaling 243 million.[31]

ZPG also sought to end illegal migration by a combination of employer sanctions, tough border enforcement, increased labor law enforcement, and foreign aid focused on fertility control and job creation in sending countries.

Organized labor and population groups see themselves as allies in their campaigns against illegal migration.

ZPG has been joined by other population and environmental groups. The Environmental Fund, for example, has issued two reports related to immigration. The first, prepared in April 1978 by Wilson Prichett III, projected a US population of 428 million by the year 2000, almost a doubling in 25 years. He estimated that illegal immigrants and their offspring would add 163 million persons to the current population.[32] The exercise is based on questionable assumptions about the current illegal migrant stock and flows, age and sex structure, and vital rates, which are lineally extrapolated into the future.

The Fund's second report attacks current governmental handling of enforcement, the blame for which is placed on the present immigration commissioner. "Most INS [Immigration and Naturalization Service] personnel know that the numbers of illegals entering this country is dramatically increasing. They also know why: inadequate laws and Leonel J. Castillo."[33] This report gives special attention to a conflict over enforcement policy between the commissioner and the border patrol.[34]

Although the primary interests of organized labor and of population and environmental groups differ, they nevertheless see themselves as allies, especially on illegal migration.

Maintaining Family Reunion and Refugee Resettlement

A third policy approach generally supports current immigration policy on maintaining liberal family reunion and refugee resettlement goals, but seeks to revamp selection procedures for achieving these goals. Proponents of this view reject the notions that immigration is detrimental to the United States and that the current policy of limited and selective immigration is unacceptable. There is agreement on a need to overhaul refugee policy, specifically regarding adoption of the United Nations' definition of refugees in the protocol to which the United States has acceded, and the use of parole power by the Attorney General to admit refugees outside the immigration ceilings. There is also general agreement on maintenance of the family reunion and labor protection goals; however, there is no unanimity on retaining all the current mechanisms to achieve these goals—that is, keeping all the family preferences at current levels or continued reliance on labor certification procedures.

The major supporters of policy maintenance and procedural reform are immigrant and refugee aid groups, ethnic organizations, and religious groups (especially the immigrant and refugee agencies sponsored by religious organizations). Organized labor is a major supporter of parts of their program, continuing the coalition that was so important for the abolition of the quota system in the 1965 Immigration Act. Support on other issues comes from civil liberties groups, employers, and publications associated with business interests.

The core supporters of family reunion and refugee resettlement goals are the voluntary agencies that developed or expanded greatly to deal with refu-

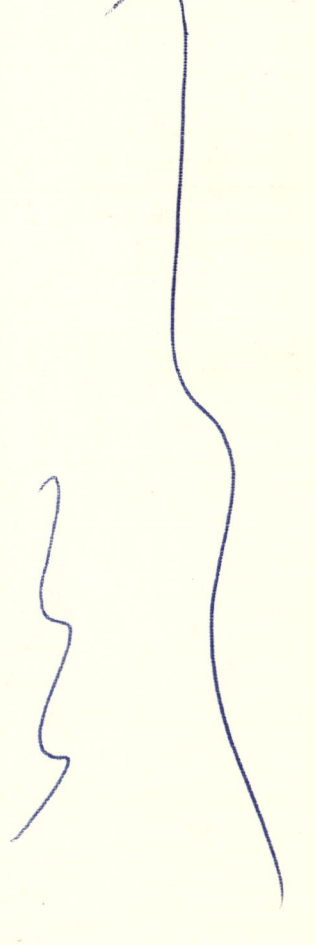

Supporters of family reunion and refugee resettlement style themselves guardians of the humanitarian tradition of US immigration.

gee resettlement after World War II. Federations of such agencies, such as the American Council on Voluntary Agencies and the American Immigration and Citizenship Conference (a coalition of organized labor, voluntary agencies, and ethnic organizations), have consistently been involved in immigration policy and programs. These organizations and their constituent members have served as private sector watchdogs and in some cases as advocates of what they perceive as the liberal American attitude toward immigration. They style themselves the guardians of the humanitarian tradition of American immigration, emphasizing the nation's responsibilities as a pacesetter on refugee policy and the contributions of immigrants to American life. They take great pride in the repudiation of the national origins quota system in 1965. Hubert Humphrey summarized their general evaluation of the role of immigration: "The most energetic, hard-working people of each generation of Americans have been those newest to our country. So when we want to put a little more zest into America, add a little more flavor to this great Republic, give it a little more drive, just let there be a little infusion of new blood, the immigrant. He is restless, he seeks to prove himself."[35]

By contrast, supporters of a stationary population and of coordinating immigration and labor policies see these groups as idealists, unwilling to face new realities and relying on historical sentiment to advocate continuation of inappropriate policy. They also detect unholy alliances of business interests, voluntary agencies, and ethnic organizations advocating self-serving policies that are not in the interests of society generally and of the least-protected Americans in particular.

As we have seen, three perspectives, which echo the historical ambivalence toward immigration, currently dominate efforts to reform immigration policy: matching immigration flows to domestic labor force needs; controlling population growth by limiting entry of aliens; and reforming procedures while maintaining current goals of family reunion, refugee resettlement, and protection of the labor force. In addition to public officials and interest groups who deal with immigration policy and its administration, the media have repeatedly directed public attention in recent years to immigration and refugee issues. The three perspectives provide useful categories within which to analyze the competing proposals on specific issues. To design minimally acceptable policy requires addressing and, where possible, reconciling these perspectives. The individual issues must be analyzed, one by one, and resolved into a legislative package that embodies a US immigration policy.

3 Policy Issues

Events often conspire to dictate policy concerns in ways that, while not literally accidental, may well be unpredictable. This has quite recently been true for US immigration policy. From two widely separated corners of the globe, Vietnam and Mexico, events have converged to sharpen the awareness of politicians and other citizens of the human side of immigration policy and of how it interacts with other concerns.

Over the past few years, all the news media have portrayed the haunting images of the Vietnamese "boat people"—gaunt and frightened adults and wide-eyed, hungry, bewildered children. Having set themselves adrift, refugees with no clear refuge in view, they have counted on the desperation of their plight to open the doors of some near or distant haven.

The images and accounts that have reached the West show these all but hopeless people refused welcome, after voyages marked by hunger, attacks at sea, sickness, and death. Their overcrowded boats, often at the point of capsizing, have been kept at bay, even while food and medicine were delivered to the passengers. America's unhappy involvement in Southeast Asia refuses to dissolve into memory so long as these haggard survivors reproach the world by their existence.

On the other side of the globe, immediately south of the American border, the panoply and seriousness of a state visit to Mexico by President Carter illustrates the importance of immigration in the overall policy context. Recent discoveries and progress in the Mexican development of its natural gas and oil resources have dictated a warming up of what has been for some time a distinctly cool and, some would say, neglected relationship. One of the most agonizing points on the agenda of the

The Vietnamese "boat people" and negotiations with Mexico make clear that immigration policy is not just a domestic issue.

talks between the president of an impoverished, mineral-rich developing country and the president of an energy-shy superpower was the question of illegal migrants crossing the border to find employment in the United States.

For years the Mexican government has been unwilling to discuss regulation of the flow of illegal migrants into the United States, considering this an essential "safety valve" for its constricted economy. Now, the president of Mexico has declared that his country prefers to "export goods rather than people" and has agreed to deal with the issue within the context of overall trade negotiations. The communique following the presidential meetings placed the points of future negotiations squarely in a context of developing-nation concerns: "the elimination of hunger, disease, illiteracy, poverty, ignorance and injustice—tasks in which all countries of the international community share responsibility."

These two events stand as symbolic and real guideposts in focusing immigration-related policy concerns. The events of the twentieth century continue to produce refugees like the "boat people," and America's tradition as a haven impels us to welcome them. On the other hand, accepting them neutralizes to a great extent the ability of population and labor-market control-minded officials to "fine tune" their calculations.

The issue of Mexican and other Latin American undocumented aliens joins innumerable other questions of North–South relations, aid to emerging countries, price protection for raw materials, and access to markets for goods produced in developing nations. Within these contexts, the following analysis of immigration policy issues and priorities can be weighed as a central concern rather than a collection of side issues.

International Migration and Population Growth

The role of immigration in US population dynamics revolves around two questions: (1) Will immigration, legal and illegal, prevent achievement of zero population growth? (2) Even if a no-growth population can be realized with current immigration levels, how long will immigration delay zero population growth, and how much larger will that population be due to immigrants and their offspring?

Ansley Coale addressed the question of the effects of immigration on achievement of zero population growth (or, more technically, a stationary population) in his paper "Alternative Paths to a Stationary Population," prepared for the Commission on Population Growth and the American Future.[36] Coale assumed for his analysis that immigration accounted for 400,000 net additions to the population. Under that assumption, if total fertility of foreign-born women equalled replacement level—that is, 2.11 births per woman per lifetime—and the fertility of native-born women did not exceed 1.97, the population would be stabilized. However, the total fertility rate for the nation is currently below 1.9 births per woman (projected from current rates to a lifetime total), and the fertility of married foreign-born women aged 15–44, according to the 1970 census, was lower than that of native-born women.[37] Therefore, at current fertility rates of native- and foreign-born women, net immigration of 400,000 persons a year is not incompatible with zero population growth.

At current fertility rates, net annual immigration of 400,000 is compatible with zero population growth.

The assumption of 400,000 net additions for legal immigration, however, seems too high an estimate, for it leaves out emigration from the United States. Robert Warren and Jennifer Peck estimated that during the 1960s, over one million *foreign-born* residents left the United States.[38] Based on this estimate, Charles B. Keely and Ellen P. Kraly estimated net additions to the population from legal migration of aliens to and from the United States at about 265,000 annually for the early 1970s.[39] Using Coale's methodology, this would mean that a native fertility rate of 2.0 would accommodate present immigration and still achieve zero population growth. These estimates do not account for the additional population losses due to *native-born* emigration.

But what of illegal migration? How much illegal migration is seasonal or temporary, and what proportion becomes permanent and uncounted additions to the US population? There is no reliable estimate of these numbers.

We can approach the question of illegal migration and population growth from another perspective. If current fertility rates were to continue beyond the achievement of zero population growth, how many net additions from legal and illegal migration would be needed to prevent population decline? Charles F. Westoff has calculated that, under current fertility trends, net immigration would have to be about 800,000 per year to prevent population decline.[40] Thus, given estimated net alien immigration of about 265,000 (and not counting native emigration, which would reduce its impact), illegal migration would have to add 535,000 permanent additions annually to the US population indefinitely to prevent the United States from experiencing population decline. There is no convincing argument that current *net*, *permanent*, *uncounted* additions to the population from illegal migration are over a half-million per year.

I conclude that claims that combined legal and illegal migration will prevent the achievement of zero population growth in the United States are unfounded. I agree with Coale's conclusion: "It is not true that continued immigration at current, fairly substantial levels implies indefinitely continued growth of the American population."[41]

> There is no reliable estimate of how many illegal migrants become permanent and uncounted additions to the US population.

Claims that legal and illegal migration will prevent the achievement of zero population growth in the United States are unfounded.

The second question refers to how many extra people would result from current numbers of immigrants and their offspring, and how long achievement of a stationary population would be delayed. Westoff estimates: "Even with continued immigration of that volume [400,000 net additions], such below-replacement fertility [from current estimates of below 1.9] means that the population will stop growing in about 50 years at about 250 million and will then begin to decline."[42]

Coale provides another perspective on this issue:

"An alternative way of examining the impact of continued immigration on a population near the stationary condition is to imagine that the native population has a fertility just sufficient to insure replacement, and consider how the population would grow as a consequence of the continued arrival of immigrants. The answer is that the growth would be at a constant arithmetic rate; that is, each year the addition to the population would be the same as in the year before—the same number, not the same proportion of the growing population."[43]

About 600,000 persons would be added per year from immigrants and their offspring combined, assuming 400,000 net immigrants, their current age and sex composition, and replacement (2.11) fertility. "At this rate the density of the American population would reach that of France (four times as great) in the year 2830, and the density of the United Kingdom (ten times as great) in the year 4970."[44]

The question of the desired ultimate size of the US population is not just one of numbers or density. Those who advocate as few additions as possible to the ultimate size of the population or even a decline below current size are primarily concerned about the consumption patterns of Americans. Americans are presented as inordinate consumers who put tremendous strains on the environment. According to Zero Population Growth, "On the average, each of us consumes four times as much grain and 37 times as much energy as a Filipino, for example." This leads to the conclusion: "There's no need for more Americans."[45]

The argument is basically demographic and environmental. Whether there is a need for or, more modestly, an advantage in having more Americans in world political or economic productivity terms is ignored. Population dynamics, then, is presented as the overriding criterion for deciding immigration levels. Depending on how great the threat of more Americans is evaluated, the acceptable size of immigration will vary. Thus, ZPG advocates a stationary US population of 243 million by the year 2008. By ZPG's projections, 150,000 net additions annually from all immigration sources is compatible with this goal. If levels remained within its demographic guidelines, ZPG would permit foreigners who marry Americans to come to the United States and strongly support US efforts to settle refugees. In other words, other policy goals could be accommodated as long as the demographic criterion has priority.

Acceptable levels of immigration vary according to evaluations of the demographic and environmental consequences of more Americans.

ZPG is one of the few organizations to present a population target, for a specified time, incorporating immigration policy. Many other population and environmental groups are still trying to prove that current immigration would prevent achieving a stationary population. What is needed at this point in the immigration and population debate is to clear the air of exaggerated claims that immigration will prevent achievement of a stationary US population. What needs to be discussed is the acceptable size of the ultimate population and a target date for achieving a stationary population.

The question is not whether we can achieve zero population growth, but when and at what levels.

What also needs to be debated is the relative priority of population and other policy goals. Should we accept delay of zero growth and a larger ultimate population for political reasons connected, for example, with refugee resettlement?

> By maintaining current policy on immigration levels, we can achieve zero growth by around 2030, with a population of 250 million.

As presented above, a net immigration of 400,000, given current US fertility and mortality trends, will result in zero growth by around 2030 at a level of 250 million. Assuming that current gross immigration of about 400,000, combined with current trends in fertility, is compatible with zero growth, current authorized levels need not be reduced. This means continuation of 290,000 visas annually plus admittance of immediate family (spouse, children, and parents) of adult citizens. The exempt group has accounted for about 100,000 immigrants a year. Since there is no foreseeable reason for the exempt group to increase and no compelling reason to delay reunion of the immediate family of citizens, I propose maintaining current policy on the volume of immigration, neither increasing nor decreasing it for population growth goals. I have accepted maintenance of current policy on volume as a working proposition in formulating the proposals on the other issues described in the following sections.

Illegal Migration

Illegal migration is an integral element of both the population and labor force aspects of the immigration debate. The topic merits extended attention because of its very nature and because it is the object of specific legislative recommendations.

Basic Questions

To understand the recent debates and legislative proposals on illegal migration requires attention to how the issue is currently perceived. It is widely assumed that illegal migration to the United States is large; is growing; is out of control; displaces US workers and negatively affects wages and working conditions; and that it produces a subclass lacking meaningful legal protection and will produce the civil rights problems and social turmoil of the coming generation. It is viewed as the result of economic and demographic determinism—that is, a large labor pool in sending countries seeking better job opportunities, coupled with the desire of US employers for cheap labor.

Illegal migration is attributed to a large labor pool seeking better jobs and the desire of US employers for cheap labor.

The number involved is probably large by any standard. Several attempts have been made to estimate the size, all of which suffer methodological shortcomings. Recent estimates by persons who are unconnected with law enforcement agencies, and who do not base their work on Immigration Service statistics concerning illegal migrant apprehensions, conclude that the number of illegal migrants in the United States ranges from 3.5 to 5.5 million. This is well below the estimates of 12 million or more that were frequently used in the mid-1970s and are still heard today. Further, we are ignorant about what proportion of this group is permanent additions and what proportion represents circular migration, a steady total with changing incumbents. It is incorrect to conclude that the estimate of 3.5–5.5 million, even if accurate, represents permanent additions to the population. Moreover, without knowledge of illegal migrants' age and sex composition and information on their fertility, estimates of contributions to future growth are sheer speculation.

Without knowing the number of illegal migrants and their age and sex composition, estimates of their contribution to future growth are sheer speculation.

The groups of illegal migrants from different sources studied to date indicate a wide variety of behaviors and intentions. Thus, almost any claim (or denial) is probably true (or false) depending on the particular stream to which reference is made. The first major problem for policymakers and public officials is determining what steps can be taken in the face of a movement, with costly domestic and foreign implications, when basic information is lacking.

It is assumed that illegal migration is growing and therefore out of control.[46] The devaluation of the Mexican peso in 1976 is thought to have resulted in increased movement toward the more valuable American dollars. Estimates made in 1974 by Alexander Korns of the Bureau of Economic Analysis[47] indicated that the major growth in the number of illegal migrants in the United States took place in the late 1960s and leveled off in the 1970s. No one has presented data, even symptomatic data, indicating that the assumed upswing in migration as a result of the peso devaluation has taken place.

> The most nagging issue is whether illegal migrants not only fill jobs for which US workers are unavailable but also displace US workers or create conditions that lead Americans to shun certain jobs.

The illegal movement, in fact, may not be out of control but be imperfectly regulated by current law enforcement practice. The most nagging issue is whether current enforcement results in numbers of workers who not only fill job slots for which American workers are not available but also replace US workers or create conditions that lead US workers to shun particular jobs. Probably all three processes operate to some degree: filling in, displacement, and making certain jobs undesirable by self-fulfilling prophecy. How much of each takes place and how to find out are unanswered questions.

Similarly, the potential for and existence of violations of the human and civil rights of illegal migrants and their offspring are clear. The potential for future problems is also clear. Both as a national policy and for the sake of the rights of migrants themselves, illegal migration is not acceptable. Nevertheless, when projecting current illegal migration as the source of the civil rights problem of the next generation, some cautions should be exercised. Such phrases can easily conjure up images of "them" rioting or causing social disturbances to attain civil rights or access to economic and social opportunity. It is hardly necessary to draw out the implications of this type of thinking, and I reject the implication that those who express concern for the civil rights of illegal migrants are purposely conjuring up such images.

In the face of all these unknowns, what policies should be adopted? Before making policy suggestions, it would be useful to review the Carter proposals on undocumented aliens. These proposals, made in 1977, embody a good deal of the consensus thinking in the government on illegal migration, as well as some novel aspects developed by the Carter Administration.

The Carter Proposals on Undocumented Aliens

The Carter Administration announced a set of proposals on undocumented aliens on 4 August 1977. They were submitted to Congress, and hearings were held before the Senate Judiciary Committee in spring 1978. The proposals were not acted on in the 2nd Session of the 95th Congress (1978), and it is not clear whether and in what format such proposals will be submitted to the current (96th) Congress. The general goals of the 1977 proposals can be outlined and analyzed to evaluate recent thinking in the Executive.

President Carter has proposed amnesty for undocumented aliens in the United States and sanctions against employers who hire them.

The Carter proposals had two major legislative thrusts: amnesty for undocumented persons in the United States and sanctions against employers who hire illegal migrants.

The amnesty program was based on the premise that any attempt to develop a massive deportation plan was both unworkable and inhumane. The program had two components. Migrants who had entered the United States illegally before 1 January 1970 would be granted immigrant status if they met the health, moral character, and public charge standards of the law. In effect, a kind of statute of limitations of seven years was to be applied. Those who had entered after 1 January 1970 but before 1 January 1977 would become a new immigration class, temporary resident aliens. No status change would apply to illegal migrants who arrived after 1 January 1977. While the pre-1970 group could assume all the rights and privileges of immigrants, the new temporary resident aliens would be permitted to work in the United States as well as leave and reenter the country during a five-year period. They could not bring in family members during that time and would be ineligible for such federally sponsored services as Medicaid, Food Stamps, Aid to Families with Dependent Children, and Supplemental Security Income. In effect, the temporary resident aliens would constitute a five-year temporary worker program. To meet the protests of local governments about bearing unequal burdens in delivery of services, the President proposed that the temporary resident aliens be counted in formulas used for revenue sharing in order to compensate state and local governments where they were living.

The amnesty proposals were criticized both as too lenient and as arbitrary and likely to foster fraud.

The amnesty proposals were criticized from differing points of view. Some criticized the whole concept as too lenient on law violators, who would be rewarded while those who followed the rules might not be able to come to the United States. From another perspective, the two-tiered amnesty system was criticized as arbitrary and likely to foster an administrative nightmare that would encourage fraud. Further, if the temporary resident aliens paid taxes, the question was raised whether it is just to forbid access to programs paid for by their taxes. Indeed, lack of access to Medicaid programs might involve public health hazards related to lack of immunization and nontreatment of communicable diseases.

Finally, the President's proposals were purposely vague on what should happen at the end of the five-year period. Registration of the temporary resident aliens was intended to produce the needed information about numbers and characteristics so that a decision could be made whether to continue the temporary status, to permit adjustment to immigrant status, or to require departure. In effect, the government proposed a bargain of five years of secure residence—with the protection of the law, the right to work, and possible permission to remain longer—in exchange for registering and possibly being required to depart after five years. This bargain met a mixed but generally negative response from ethnic organizations and immigrant and refugee aid agencies.

The second legislative thrust of the Carter proposals was to impose a civil penalty of $1,000 for each hire of an undocumented alien, with the possibility of an injunction to force an employer to cease hiring. In fact, the proposed legislation instructed the Attorney General to seek injunctions against employers with a pattern of hiring illegal migrants. The Attorney General was to publish regulations specifying what identification an employer had to see in order to establish a rebuttable defense that a bona fide inquiry had been made about the legal status of a job applicant.

The employer sanctions, as this part of the bill is referred to, were meant to cut off the access of undocumented workers to employment. It was assumed that illegal migration would decline, jobs would open up to Americans, and even that wage levels and working conditions would be improved. The sanctions, however, were criticized as too weak; employers, for example, could absorb the $1,000 penalty as a cost of doing business. The AFL-CIO advocated a criminal penalty for hiring

Fearing sanctions, employers might discriminate against persons who seem "foreign," thus jeopardizing the job prospects of US citizens and legal immigrants.

illegal migrants. In addition, the practicality of enforcement was questioned. Some said national identity cards would be needed for effective enforcement.

Ethnic advocacy and civil rights groups argued that the effect of sanctions, especially if a national identity card or work permit were required, could result in discrimination, especially against Spanish-origin and Asian groups. Out of genuine fear of sanctions or using them as an excuse, employers might discriminate against persons who looked or sounded "foreign," which could obviously affect many US citizens and legal immigrants. Thus, sanctions would provide a structural encouragement for the prejudiced and unprejudiced alike to avoid hiring certain persons—or at least require more proof of legal status from them—solely because of looks or accent. It must be pointed out in this context that it is not against US Civil Rights law to discriminate against a person on the basis of alienage. While refusal to hire aliens only from certain countries would be discrimination by national origin, an employer can legally refuse to hire all aliens. In fact, the US government discriminates against aliens in civil service employment, since citizenship is an eligibility requirement.

> Because businesses can relocate or adjust in other ways, effective employer sanctions may mean a net loss of jobs for US workers.

The major debate concerns whether even successfully enforced sanctions could protect the jobs and wages of American workers. Businesses seeking cheap labor can relocate at home or overseas or seek legislation to eliminate minimum wage coverage by age or economic sector. Relocation to parts of the country where labor costs are lower may increase opportunities for some US workers but still cause significant dislocations in the areas losing the firms and their ancillary businesses. Such dislocations have already taken place in some sectors of agriculture and in the garment and textile industries. There is also the possibility that some businesses would close. It is not altogether clear, therefore, whether a net gain or loss of jobs would result from the direct and indirect adjustments to effective sanctions.

President Carter also proposed increased border enforcement and stricter enforcement of labor laws, including the Federal Farm Labor Contractor Registration Act, which already forbids an agricultural contractor or employer to hire illegal migrants. Border enforcement was further emphasized in a border management reorganization plan developed by the President's Reorganization Project. This plan was ready for submission to Congress in the summer of 1978, but the President decided to wait at least until the new Congress took office in 1979. The plan calls for the customs and border patrol to be merged into a single border management agency in the Treasury Department. Supervision and regulation of visa issuance would be transferred from the State Department to the Justice Department's Immigration and Naturalization Service. At this point, no major policy or personnel changes regarding border enforcement have taken place.

Finally, the President emphasized the need to promote continued cooperation with the governments of sending countries to improve their economies; however, he has not yet presented specific proposals.

The Carter proposals have called attention to two areas neglected in post–World War II immigration policymaking: implications for the labor force and foreign policy. Most postwar discussions of immigration policy have emphasized the "moral dimension"[48]—such topics as America as a refuge, how assimilable immigrants are, the reunification of families, and the need for and benefits of a generous immigration policy to reaffirm the openness of

American society to new ideas and as a place of opportunity. The historical tension between protection and acceptance is reflected in the policy responses of the period: resettlement of European refugees, along with the reaffirmation of the principle of quotas in the McCarran-Walter Act of 1952; Hungarian, Cuban, and Indochinese refugee programs; and the abolition of the quota system at the same time that a ceiling on Western Hemisphere visa issuance and labor certification were imposed in the 1965 Act. However, these policy decisions were made primarily on the basis of what was considered just, equitable, or in the national interest, with little or no reference to manpower impacts. At present, reform of both illegal migration and general immigration policies focuses on the economic, and particularly the labor force, impacts of international migration to the United States.

The illegal migration issue illustrates how increasingly interconnected the foreign and domestic policy dimensions of immigration have become. A policy that is oriented toward domestic concerns and cuts off access to the job market may not only be difficult to enforce even at a high cost, but may also create foreign relations problems. Only after announcing the contours of its proposal to reduce illegal migration from Mexico did the Carter Administration fully comprehend the foreign policy implications of a course supported largely by domestic considerations. Some within the foreign policy community have warned that effective curtailment without some work opportunities for the migrants would not only be a severe blow to the Mexican economy but also could drive the government either sharply left or right, neither a desirable outcome if the United States seeks a politically stable neighbor. Moreover, at a time when the United States wants access to Mexican oil and natural gas, the unpopularity in Mexico of the Carter proposals

> The illegal migration issue illustrates how increasingly interconnected the foreign and domestic policy dimensions of immigration have become.

has done little to improve our bargaining position for energy to bolster the domestic economy. Arguably, this situation was caused by a bureaucratic snafu, avoidable had there been better communication between domestic and foreign policy staffs within the government. On the other hand, failure to consider how immigration policy will "play" in Mexico City, as well as in Peoria, may illustrate deep uncertainty, both within and outside government, about what interests are to predominate in relations with Mexico and in making immigration policy generally.

Alternative Proposals on Illegal Migration

The Carter proposals were an effort to buy time. The temporary resident alien classification and the President's proposals to review and cooperate on foreign policy, to reevaluate the current temporary labor program, and to create the Interagency Task Force on Immigration all indicate as much.

The United States must face the question of whether we need temporary labor and, if so, in what form. The need for temporary labor may have to be viewed not only in the context of domestic shortages but also in the context of our ability to absorb temporary labor, even when not critically needed, in recognition of the US interest in furthering political and economic stability by providing breathing room for sending countries that choose an employment-generating development policy. Further, the manpower effects of the "baby bust" must be evaluated. Will the United States have a manpower shortage in the late 1980s and 1990s?

Finally, we should not attribute to international migration an exaggerated effect on US unemployment. The unemployment rates in the United States are not primarily the result of illegal migra-

The unemployment rates in the United States are not primarily the result of illegal migration.

tion. Immigration should also not be looked to as the solution for labor shortfalls later in the century. Whether the United States has the data and administrative capacity to use immigration to regulate the labor market is debatable. Whether the economy is so static that unemployment can be measurably affected by adjusting immigration rates year to year is also debatable. That we should slacken our efforts to train and upgrade the native work force is socially unacceptable. However, the choice is not heavy reliance on foreign labor or nothing. There are middle positions that may be acceptable on manpower and other grounds.

US policy on illegal migration should include provisions for amnesty, a temporary labor program, and labor law enforcement.

Mass deportations are clearly impractical and inhumane, but a two-tiered amnesty program, as outlined in the Carter proposals, seems administratively unworkable. Any person who entered the United States illegally before 1 January 1977 should be permitted to adjust status to permanent immigrant. The required residence period, plus conformity to health and other immigration criteria, would indicate a person has roots in the United States and the potential to integrate as a permanent immigrant.

A temporary labor program should be developed to permit migrants to work in regions and sectors identified by the Department of Labor as in need of manpower. The Labor Department program could be carried out in cooperation with employers and labor unions, so that efforts to undercut the US work force or to claim an excess of available workers when none exists could be minimized.

Immigrant status might well be granted to a temporary worker (and his or her family) who labors in the United States between, for example, 15 and 25 months in any five consecutive years. In effect, the United States would declare its acceptance of temporary workers; if a person worked here, he could build up some rights to settle.[49]

Permitting families to accompany the workers and providing access during their authorized stay to the social benefits available to immigrants (with the exception of the right to petition for citizenship) would provide an inducement to limit the number of workers admitted under a temporary labor program. Under the tripartite cooperation of government, labor, and employers, such an arrangement would alleviate labor shortages, but not at bargain basement prices. This admittedly controversial suggestion answers the criticism that migrant worker programs split up families, expose workers and their dependents to exploitative conditions, and exclude them from benefits paid for by their taxes and productivity with the thin justification that it is better than they could get at home. Thus, genuinely needed labor could be recruited, and the migrant worker could have social and economic security as well as the tax obligations of any other worker in the United States. Since employers would have to pay prevailing wages and benefits, they would have fewer reasons not to rationalize production because of the unavailability of cheap labor. As proposed below, temporary workers who qualify for adjustment of status to immigrant after so many months of work in a given period will be the only immigrants who may enter on the basis of employment or work skills.

A temporary labor program must be backed by a major effort at enforcing current labor law that specifies minimal standards. Sanctions against employers hiring illegal migrants should be part of US labor policy, but not the centerpiece in labor law

Under a temporary labor program, needed workers could be recruited, and the migrant family would have social and economic security, along with tax obligations.

> To target labor law enforcement on hiring of illegal migrants rather than on wages, hours, working conditions, and the right to organize is to confuse priorities.

enforcement. To focus enforcement on hiring illegal migrants rather than on wages, hours, working conditions, and the right to organize is to confuse priorities. If enforcement were effectively guided by current labor law, the benefits would accrue to the total US labor force, to workers who have a right to the fruits of their labor under safe conditions. Proper enforcement in this sphere would reduce the assumed extra attraction of illegal migrants to unscrupulous employers.

US employment and manpower problems will not be solved by focusing on enforcement of employer sanctions for hiring undocumented aliens. Labor law enforcement, a full employment strategy, and manpower training, coupled with a temporary worker program as outlined—including government, employer, and labor input—are suggested as more promising alternatives. I assume also that current levels of border enforcement will continue, with such improvements as focusing enforcement efforts on areas of greatest illegal entry and authorization to seize vehicles used in migrant smuggling operations.

Legal Immigration and the Labor Force

The impact of legal immigration—in addition to illegal migration—on the labor force is a topic for debate. Currently, immigrants who wish to qualify for a worker preference (third and sixth preferences) and nonpreference applicants for a visa (see Table 2) require employment certification from the Department of Labor. (See Table 3 for a synopsis of major immigration law provisions.) The certification is supposed to testify that US workers are not available for the job in question and that the terms of employment meet prevailing conditions. The complex process involves the filing of a petition by the employer, with supporting documentation concerning the position and the employer's efforts at recruitment. The process has a number of drawbacks. Persons residing in the United States for other purposes (study, exchange programs, or even tourism) have the opportunity to scout the labor market. North and LeBel[50] cite a Government Accounting Office study that reviewed 442 certification cases. In 191 instances the applicants were in the United States, and 101 were already working at the job. Of the 101 at work, 42 had a nonimmigrant visa that permitted them to work, while the remaining 59 were apparently visa abusers or illegal migrants. The ability of nonimmigrants in the United States for education and training to adjust to immigration status also thwarts the purpose of foreign-student and foreign-exchange programs.

In fact, since labor certification is required only of persons not being admitted to join their families and by nonrefugees, it affects less than 10 percent of recent immigrants, whereas about 52 percent of immigrants are estimated to have joined the labor force within two years of arrival.[51] Labor certification is only a token attempt to protect the US labor market. Nevertheless, the concept is strongly supported by organized labor, which would oppose any suggestion to drop the program without other mechanisms to protect the labor market from undue competition by foreign nationals coming to the United States by virtue of their skills or a supposed labor shortage.

The fact that the labor force impacts of immigration have heretofore been neglected in policymaking does not mean that immigration should now be increasingly subordinated to manpower policy. The proposal to gear immigration volume to unemployment rates has the virtue of simplicity, but is a blunt instrument for tuning such a complex

> Labor certification is only a token attempt to protect the US labor market.

> Immigration policy is a blunt instrument for fine tuning the needs of the US labor force.

arrangement as the workings of the job market. In addition to assuming a fairly static job market, it overlooks the fact that it requires over one million persons to produce a one percent change in unemployment rates. But suppose, for a moment, that the job market were static and the proposed scheme were administratively possible. Since about one-half of immigrants enter the labor force, to vary immigration levels between 300,000 and 500,000 per year, as proposed by North and LeBel,[52] would reduce unemployment by one-tenth of one percent at most.

I would propose dropping the worker preferences (third and sixth) entirely. Rather than trying to move toward greater subordination of immigration policy to manpower considerations or expansion of labor certification procedures, I suggest eliminating current methods of manpower recruitment through immigration.

Each of the two worker preferences now reserves 10 percent of the 290,000 ceiling, or a total of 58,000 visas. As proposed below, about 35,000 of these could be provided for refugees. The remaining 23,000 would be reserved for temporary migrants permitted to adjust status after working for the appropriate time, for persons who make substantial investments creating jobs in the United States (at a figure well above the current $40,000 investment requirement), and perhaps (if any visas remain) for "new seed" immigrants—those who do not qualify for a preference—who would still be required to get labor certification.

The present law's potential for encouraging brain drain from less developed sending countries would be reduced. The United States would no longer be recruiting highly skilled labor through its preference system, and the number and complexity of labor certifications for immigration would decline or be eliminated.

Family Reunion

Another issue in the reform of immigration laws is the scope of family relationships that qualify for a visa preference. The major objection voiced is to the fifth preference: brothers and sisters of US citizens over age 21. If the purpose of the relative preference, critics argue, is the reunion of families, such a degree of kinship should not warrant a visa preference.

The whole relative preference system is often seen not only as smacking of nepotism but also as containing an endless snowball effect, so that resident aliens and naturalized citizens could conceivably qualify huge numbers of immigrant applicants. Given overall ceilings, however, such snowball effects are regulated.

The policy choice seems to be the degree of cultural pluralism to be tolerated in immigration policy in general and in the preference system in particular. It might also be added that family links in the United States would appear to be a good starting point for successful integration into the newly adopted country.

Family reunion should remain a cornerstone of US immigration policy. Ceilings effectively control any snowball effect. I would suggest retaining the current preferences, including the one for brothers and sisters of adult US citizens. The United States and our immigration laws can accommodate cultural traditions that value such kinship ties. Calling such family reunion policy nepotism is political rhetoric. Trying to pit national interests against family or individual interests as a policy framework seems to assume that individual welfare of citizens and strengthening the family unit are somehow at odds with other, unspecified national goals.

The preference system proposed in Table 4 would retain the current four family preferences at the level of 74 percent of the visas, with a fall down of

Family ties in the United States seem to be a good starting ground for successful integration into the newly adopted country.

The proposed preference system would increase refugee visas from 17,400 to about 50,000, without raising total immigration ceilings.

unused visas to the next category. I do not propose changes in the percentages allotted to each preference, but there is room for some shifting depending on demand patterns. The proposed preference system would increase the visas in the refugee preference to about 50,000, or 17 percent of the total, while the remaining 9 percent, plus unused family preference visas, would be allocated to migrant labor adjustments. This preference system would continue to operate within the 290,000 visa ceiling, with no increase contemplated. The admission of the immediate family of citizens outside the ceiling would be continued. This amounts to about 100,000 immigrants a year, with no apparent reason to expect an increase. Thus, gross legal immigration would remain at 400,000 per year, offset according to recent estimates by about 100,000 to 120,000 foreign-born emigrants.

Nonimmigrants and Adjustment of Status

Current law permits many people to come to the United States as nonimmigrants, sometimes for extended periods. In addition to the obvious groups, such as tourists and diplomats, are foreign students, exchange visitors, intracompany transferees of multinational corporations, representatives of the media, workers in international organizations, and highly skilled professionals in academic disciplines, the arts, sports, and so on. Many of these visa classes are permitted to adjust to immigrant status while in the United States.

The adjustment of status mechanism is a convenient and humane way to permit someone to obtain an immigrant visa without the formality of making several trips to a US consulate in a foreign country. On the other hand, the ability of those with more wealth to come to the United States to hunt for a job, or to frustrate the aims of student

**Table 4
Proposed
Preference
System**

1. First preference: Unmarried sons and daughters of US citizens.
   Not more than 20 percent.

2. Second preference: Spouse and unmarried sons and daughters of an alien lawfully admitted for permanent residence.
   20 percent plus any not required for first preference.

3. Third preference: Married sons and daughters of US citizens.
   10 percent plus any not required for first two preferences.

4. Fourth preference: Brothers and sisters of US citizens over age 21.
   24 percent plus any not required for first three preferences.

5. Fifth preference: Refugees.
   Not more than 17 percent.

6. Sixth preference: Migrant workers adjusting.
   9 percent plus any not required for the first five preferences.

7. Nonpreference: Any applicant not entitled to one of the above preferences (including investors, but not available for adjustment of status from a nonimmigrant visa).
   Any numbers not required for preference applicants.

and exchange programs by training in the United States and then remaining, complicates the role of the adjustment mechanism. The need is to retain the possibility of adjustment for the desirable reasons, while eliminating the abuses not intended by the policy.

> Adjustment of status should be limited to immediate family of citizens, to those who qualify for a family preference, and to temporary migrant workers who qualify under the proposed program.

Adjustment of status should be limited to immediate family of citizens, to those who qualify for a family preference, or to temporary migrant workers who qualify under the program outlined earlier. In this way the humanitarian intent of the adjustment process can be maintained. The elimination of worker preferences and, therefore, of the opportunity for students, exchange visitors, and other nonimmigrants to adjust status on the basis of skills or education would both strengthen foreign student, training, and exchange programs and reduce the potential of any brain drain from developing nations. A bona fide family tie, however (e.g., marriage between an exchange visitor and a citizen), could result in adjustment.

Refugee Admittance

Three issues on refugee policy require attention. The first is the definition of who is eligible for a preference visa as a refugee. The current immigration law limits refugee status to those fleeing from a Communist-dominated country or the Middle East. A broader definition, in line with the UN protocol on refugees acceded to by the United States, is needed (see Table 5, pp. 72–75). The change in legislative definition has wide backing, but passage has been delayed by disagreement over other refugee issues.

The second issue is that persons receiving a seventh preference visa as refugees are technically not immigrants, but conditional entrants: they may adjust after two years to immigrant status. The thorough inquiry on applicants for visas and preference status should eliminate the need for this additional two-year trial period. Normally, the refugee still has to wait an additional five years to be eligible for citizenship, which involves another check.

The third issue involving refugees is the most difficult. Because of the immigration law's narrow definition of a refugee, and more especially because of the lack of a refugee preference before 1965 and a present limit of 6 percent on visas for seventh preference, large numbers of refugees cannot be admitted through normal immigration channels. However, a provision in immigration law, called parole power, permits the Attorney General to allow entry for up to two years of any person whose admission is deemed to be in the national interest. This use of parole power was envisaged as an emergency measure to allow such things as medical treatment for victims of accidents at sea. Nonetheless, it has been invoked, frequently at the urging of members of Congress, to admit large numbers of Hungarians, Cubans, Indochinese, and smaller groups of victims of political persecution. There has been much uneasiness among various Attorneys General and some members of Congress about the legality of this broad-stroke use of the parole power.

Some congressional members also are unhappy with such broad administrative discretion outside the immigration policy set by a Congress that is very aware of its constitutional prerogatives. The fact of delegation of broad discretionary powers (assuming that parole in fact legally confers power on the Attorney General for such large group admissions) has been driven home since, in each case of large-scale use of parole, legislation is necessary to grant immigrant status to the parolees. Since the parole status lasts up to two years, and the original purpose of parole envisaged emergency, temporary presence with a return, no general provision exists to adjust status from parolee to immigrant. Thus, special legislation has been introduced by which Congress in effect has been asked to affirm the parole action of the Executive. Given

US immigration law requires a broader definition of who may qualify for refugee status.

the resettlement programs, the numbers involved, and the political nature of refugee movement, Congress really had no alternative but to acquiesce.[53]

The policy problem, therefore, is to devise a refugee system that (a) provides a reasonable definition of a refugee; (b) is generous enough to permit the United States to take its fair share annually of victims of war, political tyranny, or persecution; (c) is part of an overall immigration system; (d) is flexible enough for officials to react to emergency situations, but with congressional approval before the fact. This last stipulation would apply to situations that require exceeding an annual allotment for refugee resettlement but that seem to Congress and the President to be in the national interest or in keeping with a doctrine on human rights.

> If refugee visas are increased to 50,000, regular funding for resettlement activities should be assured.

Such a system could more easily be implemented if (a) the UN definition or a variation of it becomes US law; (b) about 50,000 of the 290,000 visas authorized worldwide are reserved for refugees, as proposed above; (c) admissions in excess of 50,000 refugees a year require prior congressional approval. Finally, it is not well known outside government that the vast bulk of the resettlement and integration of Hungarian, Cuban, Indochinese, and a number of other refugee groups was carried out by voluntary immigrant aid organizations, both religious and nonsectarian. Thus, not a US government agency but this extraordinary network of men and women performs the very difficult task of resettlement. The federal government has provided reimbursement for resettlement on an ad hoc basis. If the decision is made to increase refugee visas to the level of 50,000 a year, funding should be provided on a regular and secure basis for the services that these organizations, with their grass-roots, community bases, perform far better than any federal agency could.

If worker preferences are dropped from immigration law, the general outlines of the proposed refugee policy could be accommodated. Since some of the visas, freed by elimination of the labor preferences would be allocated to refugees, enhancement of the refugee resettlement goal could be achieved without increasing the worldwide ceiling. A bill (HR 7175, 95th Congress, 1st Session) similar in form to the outlines presented above has been the basis of hearings at which the Executive and voluntary agencies have testified. Although technical issues remain, a consensus seems to be developing and should be pursued, given the broad support for the American tradition of accepting victims of political repression and natural disaster.

Pluralism

The issues of ethnic political organization and language maintenance are old themes in American history. The traditional solution has been to require English-language usage, particularly through language assimilation in schools. The current policy of bilingual and bicultural education has raised again the question of language maintenance. Even further, the large number of Spanish-language residents and citizens raises the possibility of a bilingual nation. Feelings are strong on both sides of this issue.

We must reaffirm that ethnic discrimination has no place in US immigration policy. Thus, the growing political power of Spanish-origin groups, especially among Mexican-American and Chicano organizations, should not spill over into discriminatory immigration regulations reminiscent of the nativist policies embodied in the national origins quota system.

I agree with the viewpoint of North and LeBel, as presented in their study for the Manpower Com-

The growing political power of Spanish-origin groups should not spill over into discriminatory immigration regulations.

Table 5
Proposals on Immigration, Refugee, and Illegal Migration Policy

Provisions	Proposal	Differences from Current Policy
Worldwide Ceiling	290,000.	No change.
Exempt from Ceiling	Spouse, children, and parents of adult US citizens.	No change.
Preferences	As outlined in Table 4.	Drop labor preferences; increase refugee preference.
Per-Country Ceiling	No more than 20,000 visas for preferences 1 to 4 and nonpreference. Refugee visas and migrant workers adjusting would be without regard to national origin.	Under current law 20,000 ceiling includes all preference categories. Proposal would add refugees and migrant workers adjusting to immediate family members as exempt from 20,000 national ceiling.
Adjustment of Status	Limited to classes exempt from ceiling, relative preferences, and qualified migrant workers.	Current adjustment permitted under all preferences and nonpreferences. Limiting adjustment of status as proposed is not based on what nonimmigrant visa is held (e.g., prohibiting any adjustment from a student visa) but on elimination of labor- and skill-related preferences.
	Those qualified for a current nonimmigrant visa (e.g., an exchange visitor or student) would not be permitted to come under proposed migrant worker program. For example, a foreign physician coming for internship or resident training or a distinguished professor or researcher would be prohibited from entering the US under the proposed temporary worker program.	Requires conforming legislation so that proposed temporary migrant program does not become a subterfuge for gaining immigration status by exchange visitors or distinguished persons in the professions who qualify for current nonimmigrant status. The proposals envisage prohibition of adjustment by such exchange visitors unless they have a qualifying family relationship.
Labor Certification	Temporary labor program: required either for individuals or for region using tripartite collaboration of organized labor,	Organize consultation mechanism for review before Labor Department authorizes temporary labor. Temporary

Provisions	Proposal	Differences from Current Policy
	business, and the Department of Labor.	migrants admitted to work in given occupation in given region.
	Other nonimmigrants: continue current certification procedures.	No change.
	"New-seed immigrants" (applicants not qualifying for family or refugee status or under migrant labor program): if decision is to permit use of nonpreference visas for new-seed applicants, labor certification as currently required should be continued.	No change in current procedures, if new-seed immigrants are permitted.
Transition Period	Those currently registered and approved for worker (3rd and 6th) preferences and nonpreferences ("in the pipeline") could be accommodated by using proposed 6th preference until migrant workers could qualify (at least two years from beginning of program) and nonpreference numbers.	Phase out current preference system, as proposed.
Refugees	17 percent per year could receive immigrant status on approval of refugee visa (i.e., drop conditional entry approach of current 7th preference).	Increase refugee preference from 6 to 17 percent. Refugee preference receives immigrant visa, not conditional entry, which requires extra two-year wait for immigrant status.
	Admission beyond the 17 percent requires prior legislation.	Limit parole power of Attorney General to small groups or individuals who are not refugees, for emergency reasons (e.g., medical treatment). All refugees over the 17 percent authorized would require prior legislation to exceed 290,000 ceiling.

Table 5 (continued)

Provisions	Proposal	Differences from Current Policy
	Adapt definition of refugee along lines of UN protocol (e.g., "any person who is outside any country of his nationality or, in the case of a person having no nationality, is outside the country in which he last habitually resided, and who is unable or unwilling to return to, and is unwilling or unable to avail himself of the protection of, that country because of persecution or a well-founded fear of persecution on account of race, religion, nationality, membership of a particular social group or political opinion"—HR 7175, Section 2, 95th Congress, 1st Session).	Change definition in law.
Illegal Migration	Temporary labor program: approval to work in particular job category and region of country for specified period using tripartite consultation. Temporary workers permitted to bring family for work period; entitled to all social benefits of a resident alien except citizenship or unemployment benefits beyond visa; required to pay state and local taxes, including Social Security; permitted to adjust to	Temporary workers are permitted under current legislation (H-2 worker program). Develop administrative mechanisms and limits of program as proposed.

mission: "The immigration law should continue to be, as it has been since 1965, oblivious to such factors as color, religion, and language. This is the towering strength of the immigration law (which also has many weaknesses), and it should be retained at all costs."[54]

Provisions	Proposal	Differences from Current Policy
	immigrant after working 15–25 months in five consecutive years (or some variation of this work requirement).	
	Sanctions against employers for hiring illegal migrants.	Remove "Texas Proviso," which specifically exempts employment as an act of harboring an illegal migrant. Prohibit such hiring as part of labor code.
	Focus on current labor law enforcement rather than making employer sanctions the priority item.	Requires administrative decision on concentration of resources. Increased authorizations for labor law enforcement.
	Amnesty for illegal migrants who entered before 1 January 1977 (or some later date if deemed necessary for administrative purposes).	Update Section 249 of immigration law from 1948 to 1977, thereby permitting record of lawful admission to be created assuming minimal criteria are met.
	Continue border enforcement at least at current levels. Other proposals not discussed merit adoption (e.g., more focused enforcement on major ports of illegal entry; right to impound vehicles used in smuggling operations; funding for fraudulent documents laboratory and capabilities in the Immigration and Naturalization Service).	Administrative decisions on use of resources. Legislative authorization where required (e.g., seizure of smugglers' vehicles) to upgrade enforcement. Emphasis on border prevention. Increased authorization for INS.

The analysis and options presented in Part 3 result in an immigration policy that blends continuity with some marked departures from current law. Table 5 contains a summary of the main features of the legislative proposals and a brief commentary on the similarities and differences between these proposals and the immigration law presently in force.

Conclusion

The purpose of this Public Issues paper has been to review the development of immigration policy, to analyze the major policy stances currently competing to influence legislation, and to review the major issues and suggest policy options. The policy review and especially the proposals presented in Part 3 are meant to provide a fairly comprehensive legislative framework to address the reform of immigration policy.

The review indicates that there are continuities in the historical development of immigration policy. The themes of acceptance and protectionism have each been manifested throughout the history of immigrant admissions and policies. Each theme has been expressed in a variety of ways and each is reflected in the current limited but generous policy that focuses on humanitarian goals, but with regard for protecting the labor force and the health and safety of Americans.

The very persistence of the two themes, joined with the interdependence of issues in today's world, means immigration policy is complex and far-ranging in its domestic and foreign relations implications. Naturally enough, many groups maintain or have newly discovered an interest in immigration policy. The complexity of the issues, of the law and its administration; the variety of implications; the diversity of interest groups; and the emotional nature of immigration as a national tradition and core element in the national self-image, all work against coming to a consensus on even a workable, not to say perfect, immigration policy.

The nation is at a juncture where the need for review is widely agreed upon. Interest groups are aware and articulate but generally open to discussion with one another and even to compromise. How long this state of affairs will hold is hard to predict. Thus, the Select Commission on Immigration and Refugee Policy is welcome.

This Public Issues paper has been written as a contribution to the national discussion on immigration policy to be concentrated in the Select Commission. It is hoped that the discussion of issues and presentation of proposals will provide options for new immigration legislation.

Notes

1. Commission on Population Growth and the American Future, *Population Growth and America's Future: An Interim Report* (Washington, D.C.: US Government Printing Office, 1971), pp. 8–9.

2. Commission on Population Growth and the American Future, *Population and the American Future: Final Report* (Washington, D.C.: US Government Printing Office, 1972).

3. A note on terminology is in order. The term "illegal aliens" is offensive to many, while the other widely used term, "undocumented immigrants," is viewed by others as a euphemism. "Illegal aliens," like many terms in the literature on deviant behavior, tends to blame the victim and deflect attention from the structural causes and supports in sending and receiving areas. "Undocumented immigrants" assumes permanent settlement and glosses over the incidence of seasonal or term migration. I use the terms "illegal migrants" and "illegal migration": migration because the phenomenon includes temporary and permanent movement; illegal because concern centers on the legal control of international movement, whether by inspection at entry or through conformity with the conditions of a visa. The term illegal migrant is not meant to convey or connote any ethical judgment. I desire as neutral a term as possible that conveys the focus on migration in all its varieties and the focus on legal control over borders claimed by sovereign states.

4. Leonard F. Chapman, Jr., "Illegal aliens: Time to call a halt!" *Reader's Digest,* no. 109 (October 1976): 654. The author was commissioner of the Immigration and Naturalization Service at the time. The article was subtitled "The vast and silent invasion of illegal immigrants across our borders is fast reaching the proportions of a national disaster."

5. John D. Huss and Melanie J. Wirkin, "Illegal immigration: The hidden population bomb," *The Futurist* 11, no. 2 (April 1977): 114–120.

6. US Congress. 95th Congress, 2nd Session. HR 12443. "An Act to Amend Section 201(a), 202(c) and 203(a) of the Immigration and Nationality Act, as amended, and to establish a Select Commission on Immigration and Refugee Policy," 19 July (legislative day, 17 May) 1978, pp. 4–5.

7. Quoted in Milton M. Gordon, *Assimilation in American Life: The Role of Race, Religion and National Origins* (New York: Oxford University Press, 1964), p. 90.

8. Quoted in John Higham, *Strangers in the Land: Patterns of American Nativism 1860–1925* (New York: Atheneum, 1963), p. 21.

9. Marcus Lee Hansen, *The Immigrant in American History* (New York: Harper and Row, 1940), p. 11.

10. Gordon, cited in note 7, p. 89; Higham, cited in note 8, p. 26.

11. Higham, cited in note 8, p. 4. This section on nativism draws heavily on Higham. This review is a summary of his first chapter, "Patterns in the Making," pp. 3–11.

12. Higham, cited in note 8, p. 5.

13. From *The Federalist*, in Higham, cited in note 8, p. 3.

14. Sources for Figure 1: US Bureau of the Census, *Historical Statistics of the United States, Colonial Times to 1957* (Washington, D.C.: US Government Printing Office, 1960); *Historical Statistics of the United States, Colonial Times to 1957; Continuation to 1972 and Revisions* (Washington, D.C.: GPO, 1965); and *Statistical Abstract of the United States* (Washington, D.C.: GPO, 1967, 1972, and 1977). Most of the accompanying highlights for interpreting changes in immigration levels refer to legislative or judicial events. Nonetheless, the economic and investment patterns in sending countries and the United States and the effect of the four great movements of population from Europe (1844–54, 1863–73, 1878–88, 1898–1907) and their relation to immigration levels and composition are of obvious importance. On these topics, the classic work is Brinley Thomas, *Migration and Economic Growth* (Cambridge: Cambridge University Press, 1973), 2nd ed.

15. Elizabeth J. Harper, *Immigration Laws of the United States* (Indianapolis: Bobbs-Merrill, 1975), pp. 5–11.

16. Higham, cited in note 8, p.49.

17. President Harry S. Truman, "The President's Veto Message [of the McCarran-Walter Immigration Act of 1952]." Reprinted in President's Commission on Immigration and Naturalization, *Whom We Shall Welcome* (Washington, D.C.: US Government Printing Office, 1953), pp. 275–278.

18. Aristide R. Zolberg, "The main gate and the back door: The politics of American immigration policy: 1950–1976." Council on Foreign

Relations Study Group on Immigration and U.S. Foreign Policy, Background Paper No. 2, April 1978.

19. The last three senators served on the Select Commission on Western Hemisphere Immigration, which debated whether and how to impose a ceiling on Western Hemisphere visas. In a minority view presented in the Commission's report, the three senators noted that the Senate Report accompanying the 1965 Immigration Act (Senate Report No. 748, 89th Congress, 1st Session) emphasized the desirability of direct quantitative control through a ceiling of 120,000 and qualitative controls, including labor certification. The senators expressed the view that the desirability of quantitative controls represented the prevailing sentiment in the Senate. See *Report of the Select Commission on Western Hemisphere Immigration* (Washington, D.C.: US Government Printing Office, January 1968), pp. 15–21.

20. Roy P. Fairfield, ed., *The Federalist Papers: Essays by Hamilton, Madison and Jay* (New York: Anchor Books, 1966), 2nd ed., p. 160.

21. Speech presented at the Annual Conference of the American Immigration and Citizenship Conference, 13 May 1977. Quoted in *AICC News* 23, no. 2 (17 June 1977): 3.

22. David S. North and Allen LeBel, *Manpower and Immigration Policies in the United States*. Special Report No. 20 of the National Committee for Manpower Policy (Washington, D.C.: National Committee for Manpower Policy, February 1978). North, a former assistant to Secretary of Labor Willard Wirtz, has carried out a number of immigration-related

contracts and written widely on the topic of immigration, especially its relation to the labor force, as a consultant to the Department of Labor and to the Immigration and Naturalization Service.

23. North and LeBel, cited in note 22, p. 15.
24. North and LeBel, cited in note 22, p. 225.
25. North and LeBel, cited in note 22, p. 225. Quotations in preceding two sentences are from pp. 216 and 48, respectively.
26. "Statement of Rudy Oswald, Director, Department of Research, American Federation of Labor and Congress of Industrial Organizations Before the Senate Committee of the Judiciary on S. 2252, 'Alien Adjustment and Employment Act of 1977,'" 17 May 1978, pp. 6–8, Mimeo.
27. Zero Population Growth, "ZPG looks at immigration: Questions and answers on U.S. immigration and policy," September 1978 (second in a series), pp. 9–10.
28. ZPG, cited in note 27, p. 11.
29. Ansley J. Coale, "Alternative paths to a stationary population," in *Demographic and Social Aspects of Population Growth,* ed. Charles F. Westoff and Robert Parke, Jr. Commission on Population Growth and the American Future, Research Reports, Vol. 1 (Washington, D.C.: US Government Printing Office, 1972), pp. 589–603.
30. *Population and the American Future: Final Report,* cited in note 2, pp. 116–117.
31. "A population policy for the U.S.," *Zero Population Growth National Reporter* 8, no. 9 (November 1976): 6–7.

32. Wilson Prichett III, "Projecting the U.S. population to the year 2000," The Environmental Fund, April 1978, p. 11, Mimeo.

33. The Environmental Fund, "Special report: Illegal immigration," November 1978, p. 1.

34. Robert Lindsey, "Agents criticize immigration chief as Mexican aliens problem grows," *New York Times*, 19 November 1978, p. 1.

35. Speech presented at the Annual Conference of the American Immigration and Citizenship Conference, 4 March 1965. Quoted in *AICC News* 24, no. 1 (23 January 1978): 1.

36. Coale, cited in note 29.

37. US Bureau of the Census, *Census of Population: 1970 Subject Reports, Final Report PC(2)-1A: National Origin and Language* (Washington, D.C.: US Government Printing Office, 1973), Table 3, pp. 14–16.

38. Robert Warren and Jennifer Peck, "Emigration from the United States: 1960 to 1970." Paper presented at the Annual Meeting of the Population Association of America, Seattle, April 1975.

39. Charles B. Keely and Ellen Percy Kraly, "Recent net alien immigration to the United States: Its impact on population growth and native fertility," *Demography* 15, no. 3 (August 1978): 267–283.

40. Charles F. Westoff, "Marriage and fertility in the developed countries," *Scientific American* 239, no. 6 (December 1978): 57.

41. Coale, cited in note 29, p. 599.

42. Charles F. Westoff, "Some speculations on the future of marriage and fertility," *Family Planning Perspectives* 10, no. 2 (March–April 1978): 79.

43. Coale, cited in note 29, pp. 598–599.
44. Coale, cited in note 29, p. 602.
45. ZPG, cited in note 27, p. 1.
46. ZPG, cited in note 27: "The growing volume of illegal migration may make it impossible to stabilize the U.S. population...." The Environmental Fund, cited in note 33, p. 1: "Former INS Commissioner Chapman repeatedly told the Congress that the trickle of illegal aliens entering the country in 1965 has rapidly become a torrent of such size and force that the INS was helpless to stop it. In the last two years the numbers have doubled." Also see testimony of Doris Meissner, deputy associate attorney general, in *Hearings Before the Select Subcommittee on Population*, No. 5 (Washington, D.C.: US Government Printing Office, 1978), p. 301: "Illegal immigration is significant and growing."
47. Alexander Korns, "Coverage issues raised by comparisons of CPS and establishment employment." Paper presented at the 1977 meeting of the American Statistical Association.
48. See Zolberg, cited in note 18, for the development of this analysis.
49. Some attention should also be given to proposals for an international compensatory facility for development to help defray the cost to poor sending countries of raising and educating manpower. Two proposals for such labor compensatory facilities are outlined in HRH Crown Prince Hasan bin Talal, "Address to the 63rd Session of the International Labor Conference," in ILO, *Provisional Record*, No. 14, International Labor Conference, 63rd Session, Geneva, 10 June 1977; and W. R. Bohning, "Compensating countries of origin for the out-migration of their people,"

World Employment Programme, International Labor Organization, Working Paper No. 18, December 1977.

50. North and LeBel, cited in note 22, p. 58.

51. North and LeBel, cited in note 22, p. 56. On the problems of US data on immigration, particularly as they relate to labor force information, see S. M. Tomasi and Charles B. Keely, *Whom Have We Welcomed? The Adequacy and Quality of United States Immigration Data for Policy Analysis and Evaluation* (New York: Center for Migration Studies, 1978), esp. Ch. 6. See also Ellen P. Kraly and Charles B. Keely, *Handbook of Federal Statistics on Immigrants, Aliens and the Foreign Born* (New York: Center for Migration Studies, forthcoming, 1979).

52. North and LeBel, cited in note 22, p.11.

53. In the 95th Congress, PL 95-412 authorized adjustment of status for all parolees admitted through 1979. Congress therefore anticipated parole adjustment needs for one year. It is presumed that the vast majority of beneficiaries will be Indochinese refugees. Currently, decisions on the use of parole authority are made after consultation among Executive officials and members of Congress whose committees handle immigration legislation.

54. North and LeBel, cited in note 22, p. 11.

CHARLES B. KEELY has been on the staff of the Population Council's Center for Policy Studies since 1977. For many years his research has focused on US immigration policy and its demographic and labor force effects, as well as the adequacy of data supporting policy analysis. He undertook background research in 1972 for the Commission on Population Growth and the American Future. In 1978 he served as a member of the Council on Foreign Relations Study Group on Immigration and Foreign Policy and the National Academy of Science's study panel on the 1980 census. He presently serves as chairman of the Subcommittee on Immigration Statistics of the Population Association of America. His current research includes an examination of the movement of migrants between developing countries in Asia and the oil-exporting countries of the Middle East. He holds a Ph.D. in sociology from Fordham University.